BEYOND REASONABLE DOUBT

BEYOND REASONABLE DOUBT

Investigating Crime in the Raj

RANJIT MISHRA

Srishti
PUBLISHERS & DISTRIBUTORS

Srishti Publishers & Distributors
A unit of AJR Publishing LLP
212A, Peacock Lane
Shahpur Jat, New Delhi – 110 049
editorial@srishtipublishers.com

First published by
Srishti Publishers & Distributors in 2021

10 9 8 7 6 5 4 3 2

This is a work of non-fiction, based on the author's research and experiences in the Indian Police Service. It takes into account true cases that were investigated during the British Raj.

Printed and bound in India

Dedicated to
my wife Prachi Pallavi,
son Aakarsh and daughter Devanshi.

Contents

Acknowledgement

First and foremost, I would like to thank every police personnel I have ever worked with during my fourteen years of service in the Indian police – right from the instructors at Sardar Vallabhbhai Patel National Police Academy, Hyderabad to those in various districts of Bihar. They have taught me about the finer nuances of criminal investigation and also that investigating a crime is an art. It cannot be understood by reading a report; it has to be practised and perfected.

I would also like to thank the various lawyers and judges with whom I have interacted in professional capacity. The experience with them may have been good or bad, but the teachings were always invaluable.

Thanks to J.D.B. Gribble for his master work *Outlines of Medical Jurisprudence for Indian Criminal Courts,* which is like an encyclopaedia of forensic examination of criminal cases. Though more than 140 years old, this work has been my constant companion in the last seven years.

I also acknowledge the sources of stories in my book which have been inspired by real crime cases given in *A Digest of Indian Law Cases: Containing High Court Reports, 1862-1900*, by Joseph Vere Woodman, India Calcutta High court, India High Court (Calcutta, India), Emile Henry Monnier, Great Britain Privy Council, Judicial Committee; *The Digest Of Criminal Cases Vol XI*,

(1914), Calcutta High Court; and *The Trial of Criminal Cases in India*, by A. Sabonadiere (1926).

Heartfelt thanks to everyone in my publishing team, without whom this book would not have been possible. Special gratitude to my editor Stuti, who painstakingly read through the manuscript and shaped it to its best version. My sincere thanks to my publisher Arup Bose for being a friend and a guide all through the journey for this book to see the light of day.

And above all, I would like to thank my wife Prachi Pallavi for her love and constant support, for all the late nights and early mornings, and for keeping me sane, not only for this book but through my entire police life. Thank you for being my best friend and for our two wonderful kids, Devanshi and Aakarsh, who mean the world to me. I owe you everything.

Preface

Beyond Reasonable Doubt: Mysteries from the Raj is a compendium of gruesome crimes from the British period in India that are captured from the eyes of Salman Curtis, an Anglo-Indian who has been appointed in the police forces in Calcutta. As he takes a leap of faith and travels from the suburbs of London to India, the country where he was born, he participates in a series of investigations that challenge his perception and broaden his understanding of legal machinery.

Salman learns a lot as he goes from one posting to the other, and documents the cases in his journal.

The cases in this volume, with certain exceptions, have been either investigated by him or narrated to him. They are chosen as types and illustrations rather than as eccentricities and abnormalities. These are all actual reported cases from the court records of the period. Some of these cases and proceedings still form the basis of current-day investigations. Changes have been made only to make these cases more comprehensible for those not having a legal background. Anyone who is directly or indirectly associated with criminal cases in present day India will certainly appreciate that most of the cases in this volume are not very dissimilar to those being reported in criminal courts even to this day, particularly in the rural areas.

It is noteworthy that a very large proportion of cases of violence arise out of hot blood, ungovernable temper and the natural inclination of many in rural areas, who are generally miles away from the nearest police station, to take the law into their own hands and to fight it out on the spot. No magistrate or judge knows anything about the antecedents of those who are brought before him, or of their life and character, unless a previous conviction stands against someone.

Snakebite and fever are believed to cloak many deaths from poisoning, and from other causes, which are never heard of by the authorities. Many cases of false charges, of wilful perjury, and of subornation of perjury pass unpunished. Few tribunals intervene with much frequency with a view of punishing the perjury which is rife in all courts.

The objective of this book is not merely to interest the students of criminology or to illustrate the difficulties of police investigation, and of the whole course of criminal administration in India, but to try to throw some light upon the life and mentality of the ordinary people.

Lord Haldane developed the view that if law in its full significance is to be appreciated, larger conceptions than those of the mere lawyer are essential.

In modern terminology, we call this the 'public opinion'. If one were to go strictly by the rules of law, if the evidence of the principal witness for the prosecution breaks down, the case as a rule, breaks down with him. If one were to be guided by such circumstances, it would be difficult to convict in many clear cases. The simplest and most straightforward cases are constantly tainted with palpably untrue statements and inconsistencies. Where affirmative evidence is called for the defence, usually in support of the popular alibi, the matter is worse. In a word, the court is often driven to construct a new story for itself by piecing together what is acceptable, and to find facts establishing a case which differs fundamentally from either that of the prosecution or that of the defence.

Moreover, making false charges is a hobby for many in rural areas. They think that their best chance of damaging their enemies is to bring them to court. To these men, the ties of blood and caste, and the attractions of getting more money prevail over justice. They hold it no sin to give false information or to perjure themselves for the defence if a caste-fellow is accused.

A man once took a small boy out into the jungle and left him dead. Then, he returned home with the bangles the boy had been wearing. The boy, however, recovered consciousness and was able to describe and name his assailant. The police was not satisfied and, in turn, put up two witnesses to say they heard the boy scream and saw the accused escaping. But, they both made a bad mistake about the time. The accused was able to call convincing evidence of his presence in another town when two apparently respectable witnesses had seen someone attacking the boy several miles away. So, a really clear case was ruined by 'police padding', as it is called.

There is a well-known and authentic story, which is worth repeating. A complicated report of cattle-trespass was made to a young European magistrate to initiate criminal proceedings. The conscientious young man visited the village to have a view. He found that one side had no cattle, and the other had no land!

More serious are the astounding forgeries of birth registers, deeds and other documents, in cases involving property. But this form of crime is more of a local industry, with its schools and apprentices and wholesale dealers found mostly in urban or semi-urban areas.

An old Persian proverb, memorised in the vernacular by alliteration, attributes crime to three sources – land, woman and gold. Anyone with experience in dealing with crime may classify them broadly under seven heads:

1. Dacoity or robbery with violence – Often accompanied with rape by armed bands at night who are raiding helpless villagers.
2. Agricultural battles – Waged in hot blood, generally over disputes about irrigation, and cattle trespass.
3. Communal riots
4. Village vendettas
5. Mysterious murders – Arising out of cold-blooded conspiracies and ambushes, in which well-to-do people are often involved for various reasons and which are extremely difficult to unravel.
6. Child murders – For the cheap jewellery which parents insist on putting on their children; or committed by hysterical mothers who, after a domestic quarrel, will jump down a well with a baby in arms, intending suicide, but more often killing the child and saving themselves.
7. Poisoning – Generally for the sake of an inheritance, or for some petty theft.

The trials of cases in court and the various stages of the police investigation are of extraordinary interest, as the readers will appreciate from the stories which follow.

Introduction

Salman Curtis, sitting in his dimly-lit office room, could no longer concentrate on the brown pages of the ledger in front of him. He had just received a telegram which said, "Appointed in Police – start at once".

Even a dozen more words to this message could not have made it more meaningful for him. For the last two years, since leaving school, he had pestered every relative and friend he had in India to find him some employment there. Sitting in the dingy rooms in London suburbs, he had been brooding on his hard fate that was brought on due to lack of funds. He could have chosen a life in a city office or that of a soldier, but he always wanted to go back to India, the country where he was born. His mother was an Indian who had died of jungle fever when he was three and his father had soon returned to England as a sick and heart-broken retired army major.

Salman was never fully accepted by his father's relatives. After his father's death, he was almost alone. One of his school teachers had obtained for him a so-called cadet-ship in an Austrian Cavalry Regiment, but he really wanted to go to India. The telegram he had received was from a distant cousin, eleven years senior to him, who was an influential officer in Calcutta, in whose house he knew he would be welcome. In those days, a police job in India could only be obtained by nomination, as there was no provision of any examination, qualifying or competitive.

With the telegram in his pocket, Salman set out for the head office of the firm where he had been working for the last eight months. Requesting an interview with his employer, he tendered his resignation. He then, went to his family bankers and showing them the telegram, requested some advance money necessary for his passage and outfit. They readily advanced a loan with a cheque book as to draw on them up to £150. To someone whose annual income had hitherto amounted to less than £40, this seemed a princely fortune. Spending £68 for a berth in upper class cabin of a decent enough steamer to Calcutta, and £40 at an East India outfitter for suitable clothes, he still had enough to survive in India for the next three months, or so he thought.

Salman had nobody to bid adieu to in London, nor did he have many friends. Six days after he received that telegram, he was a part of the crowd on the deck of the steamer en route to Calcutta.

The days of the voyage passed quickly and on one hot, steamy June morning, Salman found his steamer proceeding slowly up the Hooghly to Garden-Reach, where the usual crowd of passengers' relatives and friends, agents, touts and peons, had gathered to greet the new vessel from England. In this crowd stood a tall young man, dressed in blue and gold, who – having discovered Salman by some mysterious means – came up and after customary *salaam,* enquired in broken English if he was "Kartis Sahib".

Salman replied that he was. He then, handed Salman a letter which was from his cousin, telling him to put himself in the hands of the bearer, Golan Ali. Soon, Salman was on his way to his cousin's house on a *ticca gadi* – the four-wheeler of Calcutta in those days.

•

Salman stayed with his cousin at Calcutta for a few weeks and then, had to report to Bhaggulpore (present day Bhagalpur in Bihar) to join as an apprentice. He boarded the first available train at Howrah and by next evening, landed at Bhaggulpore railway station.

A *dak gadi* (literally, mail-carriage) to which two ponies were attached, was drawn up outside the station. Seated on the driver's seat was a long-haired, weird-looking individual who, upon seeing Salman approach, jumped off his perch and with a profound salaam, handed him a crumpled note. It was an invitation from the district police chief to come straight to his house and put up there till he could find one for himself. Thrown from side to side and expecting every moment to be capsized, Salman survived the forty-five-minute ride on dak gadi to the bungalow of the Superintendent of Police.

The next morning, Salman was up by dawn. Chota-Ḥazri with his hospitable senior, accompanied him to the parade ground to attend the morning drill. As he approached, Salman saw a large body of men who were armed with carbines and bayonets. Clad in the picturesque blue and red uniform of the force, they presented a very smart and soldier-like appearance. In addition, there were half-a-dozen squads of recruits in various stages of ignorance and inefficiency.

Suddenly the parade drill instructor gave a war cry of "Billing sthopgiringgrong" and "Comenshelaf pot". These were words Salman had never encountered. Then, he remembered his cousin telling him that, for the uninitiated, parade ground language is apt to be obscure at times. He asked no questions. But, the Superintendent noticed his bewilderment and explained that drill instructors, often being illiterate men, learnt their drill by rote. And, the strange words

Salman had just heard were intended to represent "Balance step gaining ground" and "Commence left foot."

After an hour spent on the parade ground, they returned home to a tub and breakfast. At 12:00 p.m., the duo drove to the police office, where Salman was duly initiated into the intricacies of police work. Having little knowledge of the local language and the official routine, he sat lost in amazement at the mass of vernacular papers placed before his chief and the rapidity with which he disposed them. At 5:00 p.m., the two knocked off work and went home. Then, hastily swallowing some tea and toast, they proceeded to the Judge's house where they played tennis and billiards.

This remained Salman's daily life for the next six months, except an hour or so each day with the *moonshee*, or the language instructor.

•

The next few months went by uneventfully. He passed his examination and was beginning to be of some assistance to his chief when one morning, he received orders from headquarters, posting him to the charge of a sub-district force many miles away.

Salman decided to leave the next morning, and as the place to which he was appointed was not connected by any railway line, his only means of reaching there was by *palki dak*, a slow and unpleasant mode of transportation. Journeys by palki or palanquin were only preferred at night. So, he started late in the evening. A palki of a superior quality was specially borrowed for his use. The interior comprises a small but comfortable bed that looked inviting enough. The clean white sheets and pillows suggested ease and comfort. But appearances could be deceptive, as Salman would learn soon. After the customary farewell, he managed to crawl into the little box. The bearers put their shoulders to the pole and gave one mighty heave. The palki swayed from side to side and then, they were off.

For the next five miles, the discomfort Salman endured baffled all description. The quick, jerky motion of the palki, the weary chant of the bearers as they shuffled along at a pace that was neither walk nor run. The dust kicked up by their feet increased the stifling heat. But worse were the fumes from the *mashal* - a primitive sort of torch composed of filthy rags bound a round a bamboo stick.

Salman had barely managed to sleep when he was awakened by a violent bump. He found the palki on the ground with all the bearers congregated around it, shouting loudly and evidently more excited. After some time, he was informed that a tiger had just crossed the road in front of them. As the road at that point was a mere clearing through a dense jungle, it was quite possible that some wild animal had crossed it, though he was inclined to doubt the fact. The men, however, seemed so panic-stricken that to give them confidence, Salman fired a shot with his revolver in the direction where they said the beast had gone.

But this did not boost the morale of the bearers. There were still strange sounds so finally, it was decided to spend the night there, and move on only after day broke. The night passed without further adventure and shortly after sunrise, they reached the rest house, where they relaxed for the day. The second night's journey was through cultivated area. Finally, on the third day, they reached their destination. The only other European in the place was the assistant magistrate, Barclay, whose house Salman was to share. The two soon developed a bond and eventually, Salman eased into his life as a police officer in India.

•

A few days later, one fine afternoon, Salman decided to pay an unannounced visit to one of the police stations within his jurisdiction. As soon as he reached the police station, a middle-aged man came in and reported that his brother had been brutally assaulted by three people whom he subsequently named. The scene of the crime was only some five miles away, and although the man had been attacked the previous night, it was now late in the afternoon. It so happened that the officer-in-charge of the police station was out on duty as a minister was visiting his police station limits. Salman, the young Assistant Superintendent of Police realized that this was a one of a kind opportunity to investigate a case by himself.

He told the head constable clerk at the police station to record the man's statement in the First Information Book, or the general diary, as is required by law and the orders of the government. The clerk very nervously replied that it would be unwise to do that as the story was probably concocted. The SHO would have visited the scene of the murder to find out the facts before committing anything to paper.

Salman realized that the clerk was acting in good faith, seeking to circumvent the difficulties which distrust had placed in the way of the police. He questioned the middle-aged man very closely and found that he stuck to his story very rigidly. He could not but agree with the clerk that it was probably a concocted story, and that the delay in making the report lent credibility to this suspicion.

The man said that he and his three cousins were sleeping at a hut in their fields with the injured man, when they were awakened by a noise. They saw the accused striking him with axes. His head was cut open and he could not be alive.

Salman had his statement recorded at the police station and left for the scene of crime. When he arrived, he found over a dozen people sitting at the hut, waiting for the police to come. The injured man had been taken to the hospital. The three cousins – one of them a girl - corroborated the complainant in exact detail word for word. This level of accuracy heightened the suspicion.

The bed on which the injured man named Janu had been sleeping in the hut was soaked in blood. Salman said to the crowd in general, "There is a lot of blood on the bed and it must have dropped through to the ground. But, the ground below it shows no sign of blood."

"Yes," said an old woman with a nod of approval. "That is true, Sahib."

"When the attack was made, the bed was obviously not here," said Salman.

"True," replied the chorus.

"Then, where was Janu when he was attacked?" asked Salman.

"In the corner of the nearby field," said one of the men.

"Come, let us see the place!" said Salman, starting to move towards the next field, signalling to the man who had spoken to lead the way. The 'eyewitnesses', looking very glum, followed.

•

When he reached the spot, Salman found that the injured man had evidently lost a great deal of blood, as the dry grass was soaked in it. Three human teeth were lying on the ground in the sunlight. This was because one side of Janu's face had been cut away by sharp-edged, long-hafted axes, leaving the brain and the inside of the mouth exposed.

"You see," Salman said to the eyewitnesses present, "your story will not do. You could not have seen the attack from where you were sleeping. Now, you must tell me the truth."

He sat down on the ground. "Sit down," he said to the people. "We will talk it over."

The faces of the eyewitnesses changed, a look almost of relief coming over them. One of them said, "It is true. We made up the story to bring our enemies to justice. We are sure they did this."

"*Hujoor,* be our judge," said an old man. "Give us justice by punishing those who have slained our son."

"We must hear the truth," Salman said in a stern voice.

From there on, they collectively told him a long story of rustic intrigue, illicit love, quarrels and threats culminating in the attack the previous night. No one knew exactly which members of the other party had been involved in the killing. Salman pointed this out.

A man who had been sitting in one corner spoke up and said that he had seen Bacchu and Mayanand running away from the scene of crime during the night. He had woken up to scare away some wild pig which had come to damage his crop. He had not seen Walu, the third man originally mentioned by the complainant. He did not learn of the crime until he returned from another village during the afternoon.

His story seemed true. It was subsequently confirmed by other evidences. Blood-stained axe hafts belonging to Bacchu and Mayanand were found in a ditch and heavy bloodstains were found on their clothes. Walu was able to provide an irrefutable alibi of being in another village in a marriage ceremony at exactly the same time. Bacchu and Mayanand were ultimately convicted.

Young Salman was deeply moved by Janu's mother's appeal, and the way in which all these simple and likable people had told him the truth. They had considered him as one of their own and discussed the matter. At that moment, he felt that all the elaborate criminal justice system – with its penal codes, lawyers, courts and judges – was a little unsuited to the needs of these simple people.

The SHO of the police station arrived as Salman finished hearing what the people had to say. He told him what had happened. At first, the SHO was rather doubtful about sending a case before the courts based on evidence which contradicted the first information report. His experience had taught him that the courts were inclined to attach great importance to that first information report document. Once the investigation began, the police could have any number of reasons to tamper with the evidence. When the case went up for trial, the court accepted the evidence and sentenced the murderers.

This case taught the young police officer about some of the obstacles in the way of a successful prosecution of criminals. Gradually, he experienced difficulties that arise from witnesses withdrawing in court from statements which they have made to the police. (In India, statements made to the police cannot be admitted as evidence in a court of law.) Other difficulties arose from delay in the disposal of cases before the courts.

As Salman grew in his service and experience, he began to understand the glaring gaps in various tiers of the criminal justice system. He could feel a vicious cycle arising out of failure to bring murderers to justice. It was the vicious cycle of distrust. The courts in India somehow believe that the police cannot be trusted. They manufacture evidence or improvise upon it to fulfill their vested interests.

The courts would discharge an accused unless the evidence is 'cast-iron' and overwhelming – beyond reasonable doubt. People have learned that the courts operate that way, so they try to ensure that abundant evidence is forthcoming against the enemy.

The police are then, confronted by a dilemma. They can say that the only evidence produced before them by the relatives, purporting to be the evidence of eyewitnesses, is false. If they do so, they will be assailed from all sides and accused of corruptly failing to prosecute a murderer. They can accept the evidence and fit in with it other evidence of a circumstantial nature or otherwise as may be available. If they do so, discrepancies which will be brought out by a competent counsel for the defence. They will be blamed for concocting a false case. This is not a fanciful dilemma.

The stories that follow are real reported crimes that Salman encountered in his career as a police officer in India during a span of over thirty years.

1

Gaurang's Revenge

In a village, not very far from the Bombay port, lived Gaurang Patel. He was a handsome young man and a devoted son. Almost twenty-seven years of age, Gaurang was a tall and well-built young man with a reputation of being fair, frank and intelligent. He was the only son of Navrang Patel, one of the biggest cotton cultivators of the region. He had lost his mother at a young age, but his father ensured the best possible education for Gaurang within their village. He was married and had a two-year-old son named Bhau, whom he loved more than anything else in this world.

Navrang was almost retired, having relinquished all his professional responsibilities to his only son. He used to spend his days with his grandson, and evenings with his friends, drinking. His wife had been dead for several years now and, in spite of his wealth and social status, he had never thought of marrying again.

•

In the nineteenth century, the most important trading item was cotton, which was mostly exported to England as a raw material.

England had a huge textile industry base and its requirement for cotton was immense.

But during the American Civil War (1861-65), cotton supplies to British textile mills from the United States dwindled. As a result, India began supplying over 90% of total cotton imports in 1862-63, which led to a sudden boom in cotton prices and brought untold riches to cotton farmers in the region around Bombay.

Gaurang benefitted tremendously from the sudden jump in cotton prices. It brought untold prosperity to the region, and the cotton cultivators, who had hitherto been hand to mouth, suddenly found themselves possessed of wealth beyond their wildest imagination.

But then, wealth often comes with its own share of problems. How to spend such a huge amount of money? The answer to this question had become a big problem for the cotton cultivators of the region!

Having laden their womenfolk and children with expensive clothes and ornaments, having turned their humble dwellings into impressive buildings and having acquired much land and cattle, most cultivators were still left with surplus money to get into indulgences of all sorts. Extravagance in matters of bullock carts and trotting bulls were the most common sight. Silver-plated yokes and harness studded with silver mountings was the fashion of the day. Some even acquired silver tyres for their bullock carts.

There were many who took to drinking. Not country liquor, but British brandy, gin, rum, whiskey and even champagne. The number of shops selling foreign liquor increased threefold in Bombay. And there sprung a strong black market of foreign liquor through which liquor bottles from army canteens would find their way to rural areas.

Belonging to this category was Navrang Patel. His evening merry making would start in the afternoon and would go well past midnight. He was rarely seen sober in the last few months of his existence. Excess indulgence ultimately claimed his life and one fine morning in April 1865, he was finally laid to rest. But, this was not before Navrang had turned Gaurang into a complete drunkard too.

After Navrang's death, as a true devoted son, Gaurang would follow the footsteps of his deceased father and spend most of his day drinking. The rest of the day was spent squabbling with his wife.

By this time, the American Civil War was over and the price of Indian cotton had crashed. The cost of Indian cotton in 1859 was two annas and seven pice per pound, which had jumped to eleven annas and five pice in 1864. Proportionately, the cost of living had grown up, including the labour cost. Monthly wage of a coolie rose from five rupees twelve annas in 1860 to thirteen rupees eight annas in 1865.

But, as soon as the American Civil war ended in March 1865, the blockade of the southern ports ended and American cotton was once again freely available for the British textile mills. The cotton prices in India fell back to the pre-1859 levels.

•

Three years that followed were disastrous for the cotton cultivators in the region around Bombay. The prices had gone down; the next couple of seasons experienced bad rainfall culminating into the Great Famine of 1876-77, which was followed by rat plague. Gaurang also found himself heavily in debt of the local money lenders, the *sahukars*. To add to their woes, reckless drinking and casual extravagance which was adopted during the 'Cotton days' could not be shaken off easily.

Gaurang went from bad to worse, becoming extremely violent when inebriated, and sullen and morose during sober intervals. His wife died of fatigue and diarrhoea, leaving behind young Bhau at the mercy of his drunkard father. Little Bhau was the only one Gaurang cared for in this world. He would take particular pride in getting little Bhau dressed in bright colourful jackets, wearing silver anklets, silver bangles and gold chains. He had sold off his wife's jewellery to buy whiskey, but didn't touch any of Bhau's silver ornaments.

Bhau was treated more like a toy than a playmate by most of the village children. They had an inherent jealousy for the rich kid. But young Bhau didn't seem to mind. Perhaps, he was too young to comprehend everything. He didn't carry much airs of the rich kid as he didn't mind getting his expensive clothes soiled or torn while playing. Village women would often give him sweetmeats and other delicacies to eat out of pity for the motherless child.

•

In a couple of years, Gaurang's affairs had slipped into a state of hopelessness. All his land, which was still producing cotton, was mortgaged to the local sahukar, Devchand Shroff. His wife's illness and his reckless drinking had taken its toll and added to the misery. Only small advances from Devchand Shroff, granted as collateral against future harvest, had kept him afloat during these miserable times.

Devchand Shroff was not as bad a person as most sahukars in those days were. He had a special affinity for Gaurang as his own father had worked as an accountant for Navrang Patel for several years before entering the profession of money-lending. He was always courteous and considerate while advancing a loan to Gaurang. Devchand had a big shop in the middle of the village, just in front of his house. Little Bhau was a regular visitor to his shop and Devchand always treated him with love and affection. Bhau would spend hours sitting at Devchand's shop or playing in front of it. No one had ever seen Devchand mistreat or speak roughly to the child. And as for Bhau, he preferred spending the whole day playing around Devchand's shop, as against going back home to his drunkard father. His father's drunken violence and rough behaviour scared him, even though it was never directed towards him.

Gradually, Devchand's relationship with Gaurang started to strain. Gaurang would keep asking for fresh loan while Devchand would lament non-payment of interests on earlier loans. The discussion would almost always end in Gaurang hurling a volley of abuses at Devchand and threatening him in one way or the other.

One fine day, Devchand Shroff's patience finally ran out when he learnt from reliable sources that Gaurang had been taking advances on harvest of his upcoming cotton crop from one other money lender in the neighbouring village. On the same harvest, Devchand had already given him advances worth more than twice the amount. A stormy scene ensued between the two with Devchand accusing Gaurang with criminal breach of trust and threatening to go to the police. Gaurang retorted by vile abuses and threatened Devchand to keep in mind what damage a Patel could do to a sahukar. He also referred to Devchand as the son of his father's servant. At last, losing temper altogether, Devchand told Gaurang that if he did not settle his account within three days, he would file a suit against him without further notice.

•

For the next couple of days, Gaurang drank heavily and hardly stepped outside his room. His servants could hear occasional cries of anguish and loud abuses from his room. Bhau, as usual, spent most of the day outside his home, in and around Devchand's shop. There was no visible change in Devchand's behaviour towards Bhau. Devchand always maintained that he had said mean things to Gaurang in anger and frustration. He never actually meant to harm Navrang Patel's family and, for the sake of old familial ties, he was willing to let matters go on as before, only if Gaurang showed some fairness.

On the third night after the quarrel, it was well past midnight. Devchand's shop was still open. He was writing the ledger books of account for the borrowers. Suddenly, Gaurang appeared on the shop and politely knocked at the wooden door at the entrance. Devchand let him in. He was surprised when he saw Gaurang sitting in the corner mouthing and muttering to himself. The man's haggard, blazing eyes and suppressed manners frightened Devchand.

Alarmed, he was about to call out to his servants when Gaurang cleared his throat and spoke politely, "I have brought your money. I apologize for my rude behaviour the other day. I should not have abused you after all the help you have given me in the last few years and especially for the love and affection you have shown to my little Bhau. It was wrong on my part to take advance on my cotton crop from other money lenders when I had already promised it to you. I apologize sincerely. But tonight, I will settle all accounts. Please take out my receipts."

Devchand could sense the sincerity in his words. He took out his ledger and began calculating the total amount payable, both the principal and the interest. He deliberately paused in between to explain the arithmetic of interest calculation to Gaurang, lest he might accuse him of extorting exorbitant interests.

Gaurang protested mildly in between and Devchand, used to such haggling from every borrower, simply accommodated Gaurang's protests. Devchand was surprised at Gaurang's mild behaviour. At the end, he knocked off a good lump sum of his interest, for old time's sake, and reached a final amount which was agreeable to Gaurang. Finally, agreeing on the amount that needed to be paid, Gaurang requested Devchand to bring out all mortgage deeds and endorse them as discharged. He also requested to write out a receipt and sign it, absolving Gaurang of all debts as paid. Devchand demurred to doing this till he had secured, or at least, seen the money.

Gaurang suddenly became very indignant and stood up, exclaiming, "I am not lying. I have brought the money value. Come and see. I have kept the bag in one of your outhouses." There were a few outhouses behind Devchand's residence, next to his cattle shed. These small dark rooms were used for storing spare cattle feed.

Getting more alarmed, Devchand lit a lantern and went into the backyard and Gaurang walking closely behind him. Devchand did not like the turn of events and his sixth sense was constantly hinting at some foul play. Gaurang was walking right behind him, his head bent down, a little agitated and breathing heavily, his movements much faster than it had been since he had first made his appearance at Devchand's shop a little while earlier.

Gaurang pointed at a small room just behind the cow shed, having just one small entrance, no doors or windows. Gaurang suddenly changed his demeanour and seized Devchand by the throat with one hand so that he could not let out a cry. With the other, he forced Devchand onto the ground.

In a suppressed tone, Gaurang almost whispered into Devchand's ears, "You devil! Take your payment. I am paying you... with my son's life." And after a pause, he continued, "I have sacrificed my little Bhau and hidden his body in that heap. If you do not agree to what I say, I'll raise alarm and accuse you of having murdered him for the sake of his ornaments. Raise your right arm if you consent and quietly come back with me to your shop."

Devchand was stupefied with fear. He struggled to raise his right arm as a mark of submission to Gaurang's proposal and consented to obey him. Gaurang finally let go of his throat. Devchand was breathing heavily, trying to process what had just been told to him.

"Let's go to your shop," growled Gaurang. Seeing Devchand still lying on the floor and not getting back on his feet, he kicked him in the abdomen and pulled him up by his hair. Gaurang literally dragged Devchand back to his shop. Gaurang threatened him against making any unwanted noise at the shop and then, released his hold.

"Now you are paid! Give me the papers and the receipts," Gaurang said in the same fiercely suppressed tone.

Catching back his breath, Devchand could only ask, "What is to be done to the body?"

"We will take it away and bury it in the nearby dried up *nallah,*" replied Gaurang in a cold, calculated tone.

Devchand promptly gave him all the papers, duly endorsed, and receipts of having received the entire payment from Gaurang. The only thing Devchand wanted at that moment was to dispose of the body as quickly as possible so that Gaurang could leave.

•

Devchand followed Gaurang back to the outhouse, holding a lantern high above his face. Once inside, Gaurang immediately took out the dead body of the poor little boy from the heap of dried cow dung, wrapped in a blanket. Devchand, with lantern in his hand, led the way to the dried up nallah and Gaurang followed him.

"Take a shovel for digging," Gaurang said and Devchand complied immediately. Gaurang buried the dead body in it and a pile of stones was put on top, a customary precaution against stray dogs and jackals.

By the time the two returned, it was nearing daybreak. As they approached the village, the two separated, Gaurang assuring Devchand for the last time that he need not worry about anything.

Devchand slipped into his house, more dead than alive. He was trembling with fear, having very little faith in Gaurang's assurances. Gaurang, on the other hand, got himself drunk as soon as he reached his house. He was brooding devilishly over the events of the night, speaking to himself and tossing off cup after cup of raw spirit.

"That devil sahukar! Cannot sue and disgrace me now. I don't owe him anything. He is the son of our servant. He is devil."

But soon, Gaurang started howling and said, "How can I live without my little Bhau. What shall I do? How will I face his mother in heaven?"

After prolonged lamentations, Gaurang started planning his next course of action. "I shall blame those nomad basket makers who have camped outside our village for the disappearance of my Bhau. I shall have their tents searched and will easily slip Bhau's silver ornaments in one of the huts. Then, the body can be found..."

A few more cups of raw spirit and his train of thoughts took a different track. "Wait a moment! Why should I let that son of devil sahukar off the hook so easily? He has made me kill my little Bhau. He ought to die."

With that, Gaurang fell into a drunken stupor.

•

A few hours later, Gaurang was woken up by the servants. They all looked perturbed as they could not find little Bhau anywhere. They claimed to have searched the entire village and to have also enquired about him everywhere, but there was no trace of the young boy. Gaurang asked them to summon a few of his neighbours, all Patels. He was already working on his half-baked plan.

As soon as the Patels from the neighbourhood assembled in front of his house, Gaurang informed them in a worried voice that his beloved son Bhau was nowhere to be found. He asked them if anyone had any idea where Bhau used to spend most of his day. Everyone knew the answer. It was in Devchand's shop.

Soon, the search party headed by Gaurang was in front of Devchand's shop. As soon as Devchand saw Gaurang leading a group of Patels to his shop, he turned pale. Devchand looked terrified and it raised everyone's suspicion. Devchand could not stand on his feet and fell on the ground.

Gaurang led the search party into his house and thoroughly searched the entire house. Finding nothing, they turned their attention to the outhouse near the cowshed. The disturbed heap of cow dung in the room behind the cow shed, a shovel lying nearby with fresh earth stuck to it was suspicious enough to the entire search party. Gaurang immediately picked up the shovel and ran towards the shop. Devchand was still sitting there on the ground with his head bowed down and face sweating profusely.

Gaurang got into the shop. He held Devchand by his throat and asked, "Where is my Bhau?" A neighbour came forward and informed the gathered crowd that he had seen Devchand coming from the nallah side early that morning. All the gathered men immediately rushed towards the nallah.

•

As they reached outside the village, fresh tracks leading up to the nallah could be seen. At the nallah, a freshly laid pile of stones looked out of place. The stones were removed and fresh digging could be seen. Finally, the dead body of little Bhau was exhumed. Gaurang immediately recognized it to be that of his son.

Devchand was immediately captured and handed over to the police. No one ever doubted that he had actually strangled the poor little fellow, taken all his silver ornaments and disposed of the body in the dead of the night. Some attributed the crime to his greed for the little child's ornaments, while others attributed it to his enmity with Gaurang and their spat in broad daylight three days ago.

Devchand's incoherent protests that Gaurang had himself killed his child were considered by everyone as the ravings of a criminal.

•

Salman was amazed when he heard about these disturbing events. He accompanied his superiors who conducted the police investigation. Although, ornaments of the little boy were never found in Devchand's house when the police conducted the search, eye witnesses and circumstantial evidence left little doubt that Devchand had indeed murdered the little boy. Devchand was sent to jail, a chargesheet was submitted against him and trial began before the magistrate.

The case was so clearly made out against Devchand that no pleader would take up his case. Finally, with great difficulty, a learned pleader from Calcutta, Mr Ishwar Chakraborty was hired at great expense. But even Mr Chakraborty didn't place much credit to the ghastly story that Devchand had been relating.

How could a father kill his own son, and that too when there was no single witness to testify that Gaurang had ever mistreated little Bhau! The whole village would vouch – that no matter how useless and drunkard Gaurang had become after the cotton prices had crashed – he loved Bhau dearly. He could never harm his own child.

•

The trial began. All prosecution witnesses were examined and cross-examined. All the witnesses stood their ground and gave statements similar to what they had given to the police. They all blamed Devchand for little Bhau's death. Mr Chakraboty had nothing much to prove out of cross examination. His line of defence was merely that Devchand's guilt could not be proved beyond reasonable doubt and was hoping for leniency on technical grounds as his defendant did not have criminal antecedents. But there was not much hope. Murder is one thing, but when the victim was an innocent little boy, the entire jury appeared a little hostile.

But then, a flash of brilliance occurred to Mr Chakraborty. He pleaded before the magistrate, "Your Lordship! It appears at this current stage of trial that my defendant Mr Devchand Shroff, the primary accused in this case, is on a very sticky ground. And, in all likelihood, he is almost certain to go to the gallows. It may be considered by your Lordship as the last wish of a dying man that a thorough search of Gaurang Patel's house be ordered." Mr Chakraborty had appealed to the British sense of justice of the magistrate. The order was granted.

A search party was rushed to Gaurang Patel's house. At his house, in a bundle of his own clothes, Bhau's ornaments were found. Gaurang, in his drunken besotted malignity had forgotten to take them with him and plant it in Devchand's house when the alarm was first raised. And after the dead body was found and Devchand was arrested, police had also taken possession of Devchand's house as the crime scene. Gaurang never had the opportunity to rectify the omission. He was so assured of his plan, seeing the trial going against Devchand that he never cared to fill the gap.

•

After the recovery of the ornaments, Gaurang was kept under strict surveillance. Unable to get liquor, his nerves gave way in a few days. He finally confessed to his crime. Devchand was released, and in due course, Gaurang was arraigned, convicted and hanged.

Even till his last breath, his only regret was that Devchand was let off! And if had he not forgotten to take Bhau's silver ornaments to Devchand's house on the day of the latter's arrest, Devchand in all probability would be the one going to the gallows. Not him.

Gaurang, in his confession, had truthfully asserted that the idea of sacrificing his beloved son had never crossed his mind till the day he had the altercation with Devchand. In a state of rage, he suddenly realized what a fine revenge it would be and what an easy release from Devchand's clutches. The boy was sleeping next to him, and before he could fathom the seriousness of his offence, the boy was strangulated.

Salman was stunned when he heard the confession. He kept wondering about how the father got the strength to take away the life of his own son. Only while carrying his beloved son's dead body to Devchand's house did Gaurang have his moment of guilt.

2

The Confession

A good deal of scepticism exists among common people about the trustworthiness of confessions made by accused persons before a police officer, or while in police custody and about the methods adopted by the police to extract them.

Precautions have been taken by the legislature to secure that confessions made to the police shall not be considered as admissible evidence in a court of law, unless duly recorded using most precise and meticulous regulations before a judicial magistrate. Further precautions are taken by magistrates and judges to see that confessing persons are protected, and that their statements shall be supported by independent corroboration before they are accepted.

This protection to the accused in police custody existed even during the British rule. This, however, did not prohibit or prevent the investigating officers from taking down confessions, or for the person in custody from making one.

"Every police officer experiences in their investigating career that false confessions are sometimes made in the hope of purchasing immunity, by men who are entirely innocent. And confessions, untrue in detail, are made by guilty men. Both types of confessions are, however, false."

After the previous case came to a close with the confession of the accused, Salman's superior officer had made a statement about confession being an essential tool in investigation. Intrigued by the topic of discussion, Salman asked, "How do we differentiate between these two confessions?"

"There is a lot of difference between these two classes of untrustworthy confessions. In the latter case, they are almost invariably retracted when the accused finds that he is not going to receive a pardon, or when a lawyer is employed to conduct the defence.

"Unfortunately, in the conduct of criminal defences, a point which has once succeeded, and which has established the innocence of an accused man, such as an alibi, an untrue confession, or an attack upon the police, is seized upon by the lawyer as 'the one hope of his calling.'"

He was also told that in the past, the police had often been proved guilty of improper conduct in putting pressure upon the accused to confess. They were often guilty of what were called 'third degree' methods, and occasionally of ill-treatment. But, it would be safe to say that if statistics upon the subject were available, it would be found that these methods had been applied in the vast majority of cases to men who have something to confess.

•

Years later, when Salman was hosting a session with his subordinate officers on the importance of confessions in the investigation process, he was reminded of the elaborate explanation which was given to him.

"Every police officer experiences in their investigating career that false confessions are sometimes made in the hope of purchasing immunity, by men who are entirely innocent. And confessions, untrue in detail, are made by guilty men. Both types of confessions are, however, false."

As he asserted the statement, he was met with perplexed gazes. The group seemed to be unconvinced with the theoretical explanations and was hoping to receive some solid examples.

Assessing the need for further elucidation, he narrated the classic case of Chandra Das which was a perfect example to shed more light upon the peculiar nature of confessions.

•

It happened in the year 1916, when the First World War was at its peak. The accused, Chandra Das, was an educated fellow, with a sound knowledge of English. He had received university education and was probably one of that much-advertised classes of aspirants to clerical employment. His father had a shop where Chandra Das worked after finishing his university education. But, he aspired for a government job. His father was a good English scholar, and had many acquaintances as well as customers amongst the large English-speaking community in the city of Patna, where he lived.

Chandra Das wrote out his confession at the local police station, after going through quite an intelligible mental process of reasoning, and after weighing arguments which were quite honestly and almost reasonably presented for his consideration. Neither he nor anyone else could accuse the police of having used any physical force for compliance or to get his signature on his confession. There was a touch of humour, grim though it may be, about the way in which it happened.

•

One morning, Chandra Das arrived at the kotwali (police station) in the city and announced that he had to report the death of his wife, who had hanged herself. He was agitated and nervous, and clearly looked severely shocked. The *kotwal*, or the Station House Officer (SHO) was not present in the *thana* premises at that moment. He was out on important government business, and was not expected back for some time.

Chandra had a talk with the *muharrir* or police clerk, a very astute gentleman, well-versed in the mentality of criminals and complainants. It was his duty to enter the reports of complainants. There is a muharrir at every police station, even to this day. He has the tough job of writing out and reducing into intelligible, chronological form, the rambling statements of these complainants, until his palm has been oiled.

On this particular occasion, Chandra Das had not got very far with his sad story before the muharrir put down his pen and gave him a blank stare. Stroking his chin thoughtfully, he shook his head, and said, "The *daroga sahib* will never believe this."

The daroga, to use the term colloquially applied to the Station House Officer of a police station, is a man of great importance and authority. He is generally a man of considerable ability, splendid physique, majestic appearance and sterling character, who has risen high in his profession by sheer merit. He is continually in touch with the Superintendent of Police. He has to deal with many big situations, and what he does not know about law, crime and the affairs of most people in the bazaar is probably thought to be not worth knowing. His opinion with the average man would carry great weight, and especially so with an educated but timid man in a difficulty.

Chandra Das had done well to come straight to the kotwali, though he would have done better to have sought the advice of a male relative or a lawyer. It would have been better still, if he had happened to find the daroga in. Had he done either, this story would probably never have been written.

The muharrir had put his finger on the weak spot.

"The daroga sahib will never believe this." Seeing that he had made an impression, the muharrir went on to elucidate upon the possibilities. The poor Chandra Das would have to be detained in custody. The daroga would have to go and search the premises, have the dead body examined by a doctor and a post-mortem report made.

He added in a concerned voice, "Do you have any witnesses to the act of suicide?"

Poor Chandra Das was already crestfallen. All he could manage was a blank look at the muharrir.

"No? That is very awkward. Cases of strangling an unfaithful wife by a husband – a perfectly justifiable act – are reported almost every month. It is not even a meritorious proceeding," said the muharrir. He waited to let the effect of his words sink in.

Then he added, "If it were not for the British rule, it was by no means uncommon. Especially if the husband was unhappy and desired his first wife's jewellery. It was also quite usual for the distracted husband to hang the body on a beam, in order to simulate a case of suicide."

Chandra Das was getting the education of his life. The muharrir continued, "But if the daroga's suspicions are aroused, and he finds anything at the house to confirm them, then this might turn into a case of murder – Section 302."

This last observation, which was probably only a chance shot, went home to the fainting heart of Chandra Das. The muharrir said at the trial that Chandra Das was very pale and agitated while he was at the station. This account of what happened at the interview is taken from the statement which Chandra Das made before the committing magistrate. It was substantially denied by the muharrir. They were the only two present during the interview. Chandra Das asserted, on being assured by the muharrir that this story of his wife having committed suicide would never be believed. He asked, in a helpless sort of way, what he could do.

The muharrir then, told him that if he had killed his wife in a fit of passion, or on account of infidelity, he would not be hanged. It would be treated by the judge as a case of grave and sudden provocation, and the offence would be reduced to one of 'culpable homicide not amounting to murder'. The most that he would get would be transportation for life, and that as the British forces in Mesopotamia were badly in need of labourers for digging trenches and other works, the government of India were organising labour parties to send them there. They were taking men from the jails to fulfill the required number. All transportation-for-life men were being sent in this way, and if Chandra Das confessed to having killed his wife in a fit of passion on account of her infidelity, he would meet the same fate. He argued that it was quite an attractive proposition, and the chance of a lifetime. The men were well fed and looked after. They were first trained and then sent across the sea. He would have a comparatively free life in the open air, in new surroundings, and a new country, which he would otherwise have no chance of seeing. A large number of prisoners had already gone, and the *sarkar* had promised them that on their safe return after the war was over, their sentences would be remitted.

•

There was not much of truth in muharrir's statement. It is possible that the plan had been explained to Chandra Das later, by his lawyer or by his father. But the story which Chandra Das told would be an exceptionally ingenious one.

The muharrir – if it was true that he originated the idea – was guilty of two serious over statements. His knowledge of the defence of 'grave and sudden provocation' was not so complete as that of the average villager.

Cases occur in which the cultivator, returning to his house, finds his wife in the very act of committing adultery with her paramour, and kills one or both of them instantly. This would generally occur in the day when the husband is working in the fields. But there are more cases where although, the husband has good reasons for believing that his wife has been unfaithful, he does not catch her red-handed. Rather, he is being told by neighbours that such an incident has occurred on a given occasion. As a result, he loses his patience and nursing his grief, finally makes a murderous attack on his wife during the night.

But in many of these cases, the husband would declare that he found the two together, although it is clear that he could not have done so, and that in a fit of uncontrollable shame and rage, he put an end to them. This commonly told story was due to the general knowledge which prevailed amongst villagers that the sarkar would take a merciful view of killing if the parties were discovered in the very act, and 'sudden' provocation be established during trial.

If Chandra Das had been capable of reflecting carefully, he would probably have realised the importance of the difference between the two situations. The mistake was more likely to have been made by the muharrir. It was a grave error to make in a concocted story.

The other overstatement was that all prisoners under sentence of transportation for life were being taken. Transportation men were not drafted into parties for war efforts. The scheme was carried out with great circumspection, and only prisoners under sentence of rigorous imprisonment or hard labour were taken. But to Chandra Das, the proposal seemed sufficiently attractive. He had arrived at the kotwali in a state of great agitation and was horrified by the muharrir's incredulity. With very little capacity for well-balanced reasoning, the suggestion made to him seemed to be the better of two very unpleasant alternatives. So, he sat down and wrote out the following confession:

> *I am Chandra Das, the son of Mahendra Das. My father keeps a book shop and a general shop in the city of Patna. He often visits Calcutta in the course of his business. I was married to my wife five years ago. Her age was then the same as mine. I am now about twenty years of age. I lived with my wife in the city and worked with my father. She was not strong, and sometimes her health was not good. She did not keep purdah. She was not always obedient. We did not quarrel, but I told her she went out too much.*
>
> *For the last few weeks, I found in her box many love letters. I was very distressed and ashamed so I spoke to her about it. She got angry and said she would do as she liked. I believe she has been involved with some man. I am away from home most of the day at my shop. I did not know the name of the man. I asked her who he was, and she did not tell me. I did not speak to anyone about this, but I beat her, and she said she would not see the man again.*
>
> *Yesterday when I returned home from work, I found a letter. It was a love letter. It was in the same handwriting as the earlier letters. I got angry and told her that she would give me a bad name. I also told her that I would speak to her parents, and send her back to her parents' house. At night,*

> *I was very disturbed and could not sleep. I thought much about my troubles and wanted to put an end to my shame and dishonour.*
>
> *I did not know what to do. I had a fever and could not think. I felt mad. Just before sunrise, I got up. She was sleeping. I could not bear to see her. I tied a silk scarf round her throat and put a white cloth over her head. Suddenly she woke up and opened her eyes. I stuffed one end in her mouth, so that no one should hear her screams. She kicked and tried to struggle, but she was too weak. She was lying on her back. She did not speak so I pressed my knee on her chest, and tied the scarf tighter round her throat. The struggling stopped and she ceased to breathe. Then, she lay quite still and I saw that she was dead. I became frightened. I did not know what to do.*
>
> *First, I tried to restore her by rubbing. Then, I decided to hang the body on a beam in the room. I did that by lifting it on to a table which I dragged under the beam. Then, I put the scarf round the beam. I raised the body and drew the table away and came here to make a report that she had hung herself. She was an adulteress, but I was not in my proper senses when I pressed the life out of her.*

Chandra Das was put up before a judicial magistrate the same day and he repeated his confession to be duly recorded. The daroga went to the house and made a cursory examination. He had the body taken down and sent it to the constable for the post-mortem examination. The examination and the report were superficial in nature. They proved inadequate for a thorough investigation into the real cause of death. The report seemed to bear out the statements made in the confession.

Meanwhile, Chandra Das had communicated with members of his family, who sent a telegram to his father in Calcutta. The distracted father came at once. He could not believe such a thing was possible, and immediately sought an interview with his son in jail. He asked what had induced him to take his wife's life. He had always seemed such an affectionate husband, and had shown great devotion to her, particularly during her attacks of ill-health. Then, the son told his father that he had not killed her at all. The father was heartbroken and in tears, but the son seemed to regard the affair with a sort of philosophic indifference.

The father naturally asked why he had made a confession before a magistrate. Then, the son repeated the eventful interview which he had with the muharrir. The father did the right thing. He went to an experienced lawyer and told him the whole story. He also informed him that he was in a position to prove that the deceased woman was known in the family to have suicidal tendencies. The lawyer immediately had an interview with Chandra Das and gave him the excellent advice – an advice rarely given, or if given, rarely acted upon. He told him not to wait for the first hearing during the trial of the criminal case, but to address a communication forthwith to the magistrate. He was to elaborate on how he had been persuaded to confess. He must emphasise that the confession was untrue and that his wife had really committed suicide.

•

Chandra Das was committed to trial. It was almost inevitable after his confession, although some judicial magistrates might have hesitated. His defence had the merit of having been put forward at the earliest possible moment namely, during the inquiry before the committing magistrate. The prosecution had no evidence to tender beyond the confession and the medical testimony, except for two small facts that were proven by the daroga. The first was that when he went to the house to see the dead body, some cheap glass bangles commonly worn by women in a humble walk of life were lying broken on the floor. The second was that the deceased's jewellery was locked in a box which the accused said was his, and of which he had the key. Some argument was made upon the broken bangles, which were relied upon by the prosecution side.

It was suggested that they must have been broken in the effort made by the husband to lift the body on to the table, or possibly during the operation of strangling and suffocating his wife. The answer to this was that he could hardly have failed to see them if he was a murderer engaged in placing the body to simulate suicide. He certainly would have cleared them away if he had broken them himself before he went to make a false report.

Chandra Das was absolutely candid about them in his statement. He said that the deceased usually wore them but he could not say whether they were on her wrists when she went to bed the previous night. He was quite certain that he had never seen them broken on the floor. This led to the suggestion that they had been broken and left there by the police when they searched the premises in order to add some substance to the explanation put forward by the prosecution, which if it was accepted, might be regarded as corroboration of the confession. But the confession did not require corroboration in the eyes of the law. It was not one of those confessions which implicated anyone else, or on the strength of which anyone else could have been implicated in a charge. It concerned and implicated only the accused himself.

It was also not one of those cases in which the confession, if untrue in any of its details, was yet likely to be true in substance.

A man confessing to a crime in which others have taken part will often insert untrue details in order to minimise his own share and to emphasise the share of others. Or he may deliberately, in order to work off old grudges or to placate the police, falsely introduce the names of persons who were not there.

And therefore, it may justly be said that unless the court was satisfied of its truth in its entirety, it ought not to accept it as true at all. This is not suggested as a principle of law, nor as a rule of universal application, but as a sound working principle of plain common sense. If the man were really making a true confession of a simple crime of which he alone could have been guilty, there would be no adequate motive for inventing anything. Or to put it in another way – if you are going to act in convicting a man of a crime on the sole evidence of his carefully considered statement, you ought to be satisfied that the statement is absolutely true. It is difficult to find any justification for rejecting part of it as untrue, and at the same time, in spite of such rejection, accepting another part of it as true.

But all the questions arising from the discovery of the broken bangles were purely speculative and no inference could safely be drawn from it, one way or the other. The answer made by the defence to the second point about his wife's jewellery was that it may be dealt with later on, when the substantial defence of Chandra Das was examined.

The superficial nature of the post-mortem report did not help either side – neither the prosecution nor the defence.

There was nothing in the medical report which would enable one to decide with confidence whether the cause of death was hanging, strangulation, suffocation, or a combination of these causes. Nor was there anything inconsistent with hanging. It is often a difficult question to decide, even when all the data have been accurately recorded.

Unfortunately, the evidence was silent, because the report was silent. The report ought to have dealt with several points, if it had been thoroughly made, which became of the greatest importance in the light of the controversy which was raised at the trial. It must be conceded that the doctor who made the examination, and who subsequently gave evidence at the trial, had been told that the husband had confessed to having suffocated the deceased, and that neither the possibility of suicide or hanging crossed his mind. He was therefore, unable to add very much in his evidence to what he had said in his report. All he could do was to answer abstract questions as an expert about the usual symptoms which are seen in either case.

The presumption is greatly in favour of suicide in a clear case of hanging. One of the first symptoms to be examined should be the mark on the neck. If this is clearly defined, it will in the case of suffocation usually be transverse in direction, low down on the neck and completely encircling it. Whereas in the case of hanging, it will be higher up and oblique in direction.

When the victim is suffocated by pressure of the hands on the throat, marks of the fingers will almost certainly be left on the skin. There was nothing of that sort in this case. A common method of suffocation is to insert a *lathi* in the cloth bound round the neck and to twist the cloth tighter and tighter, using the stick as a lever. This produces a central bruise or other similar injury. The use of a soft ligature would not leave a mark. The position of the body in relation to the head is important. In hanging, the head is bent in the direction in which the combined action of gravity and suspension would carry it and is stiffened in that position. If the head is found hanging over in that position, it shows that the hanging took place before rigor mortis set in. No special observation had been made on this matter, as the body had been taken down at once by the daroga's orders and he had made no notes about it. But the doctor had noticed that some saliva had run from the mouth and that both the eyes and the tongue were protruding, the latter having been slightly bitten between the teeth.

Both these appearances are common indications in death by hanging, and the running of the saliva is not likely to be present in strangulation. In a case of hanging, it is usual to find the hands firmly clenched, and one would have expected it in this case if the woman had really hanged herself, but nothing was noted about this one way or the other.

Suffocation has been described in Taylor, the standard work on medical jurisprudence, as that condition in which air is prevented from entering the lungs, not by constriction of the windpipe, but by some mechanical cause operating externally by pressure on the chest, or by blocking the mouth and nostrils; or internally by closing the throat, windpipe, and air passages. In hanging, asphyxia takes place in consequence of the suspension of the body. In strangulation, asphyxia may be induced not only by the constriction produced by the ligature, but by the application of pressure on the windpipe.

It is also said that the indications are variable and appearances resemble death by disease that a well-informed medical man cannot always detect death by suffocation simply by an examination of the body without any knowledge of collateral circumstances.

If there was any truth in the confession which Chandra Das made, death must have been caused either by strangulation or by suffocation, or by a combination of both. It would presumably have been difficult in any case to say which. But if the case of the prosecution were true, there should have been no appearances of death by hanging. The first fact relied upon by the defence, and conclusively established, was that the deceased woman was illiterate. Not only had she always made her thumb-mark when she had to sign anything, but her family and people who knew her confirmed that she was unable to read or write. No love letters mentioned by the husband in his confession were found or could be proved to have existed. Chandra Das further stated that the story of his wife's love letters was pure invention.

The next fact was that the deceased had been medically treated for hysteria, and that she had tried to commit suicide twice. On one occasion, when she had been unwell and was excitable, she made a determined effort to put an end to herself by drowning when she was bathing in the sacred river to purify her soul. On another occasion, she had consumed poison which is why she fell ill. The fact that she had taken it voluntarily depended on the statement of her husband, but he had called in a doctor for her and had made the same statement to him at the time.

Chandra's wife also suffered from religious hysteria, and had – according to the evidence of the members of both families – developed the habit of continually washing herself. Not merely washing, but sousing and swilling herself with water at odd hours of the day. She had frequently refused food which is why she attained a state of considerable weakness. Her health and general conduct had been a source of great anxiety to her husband.

Three doctors were called in, belonging to the same community as the husband, who said that they had treated her on different occasions. They discovered that she was suffering from an aggravated form of hysteria. According to her husband, one of her peculiarities when she got excited was to throw away portions of the small collection of jewellery which she possessed. This had led him to take it from her and lock it up in order to prevent her from wearing anything but a few glass bangles on each arm and some other ornaments of less value.

Another fact relied upon rather strongly by the defence was a singular one. It appeared from the medical evidence that the big toe of the deceased's left foot had been slit with some sharp instrument, and that the wound was probably post-mortem. No one could have inflicted this except the accused, and he admitted that he had done it.

The prosecution was unable to make anything out of it. The accused, however, stated that when he first found his wife hanging, he had a latent hope that she was still alive. He had contemplated trying to take the body down, but did not know how to set about it. He also feared that if he changed the position, he might be suspected of having caused or contributed to her death. It had not been long before he realised that she was dead. But in order to make sure, he fetched a knife and cut her toe, which was the nearest and simplest thing to test, to see if the wound drew blood. He had heard of such tests being made, and it was recognised at the hearing that it was a test not infrequently practised. When no blood flowed, he knew that the case was hopeless. He added that he had intended to report this to the police, and would have done so if he had not been persuaded to alter his entire story.

It was contended by the defence, with some show of reason, that as this act must have been done by the accused, it was a strong argument against the credibility of the confession, for if he had really strangled and suffocated his wife and knelt upon her chest until, to use his own graphic language, 'the life had been pressed out of her', the cutting of the toe to see if life was extinct was entirely superfluous. It was an act which might be done by anyone who hoped that it was not yet too late to save the life; it could hardly have been done by a man who wanted to take the life away.

The jury was of the opinion that the accused man was not guilty. But the sessions judge convicted and sentenced Chandra Das to death by hanging. He believed the confession was true. He was unable to accept the story of the muharrir's intervention. He thought that, even if the wife was illiterate, she might easily have received and sent letters through a female friend. Though, it was observed in the judgement that the deceased would be unlikely to keep the love letters in her own possession when she could not read them and the husband might find them. He was inclined to think that the family and medical evidence for the defence were exaggerated in the interest of the accused, but that even if the wife had had suicidal tendencies and had suffered from hysteria, this was not inconsistent with her husband desiring to take her life, and it might have been his dominant motive.

This verdict was reversed on appeal by the High Court, who took the view that the confession was definitely shown to be untrue and that the explanation given by the accused must be taken to be a true one. The appellate court considered the advisability of asking for further medical evidence, but decided eventually that in the absence of certain material facts, no expert could do more than give theoretical evidence, and that no additional evidence as to the appearance of the corpse was obtainable.

Although men condemned to death by a single judge bench are not infrequently acquitted by a court of two-judges on appeal, the case of Chandra Das presents a striking example of a trial for murder, in which the accused, mainly on his own confession, was found guilty in a reasoned judgment by a single judge. In which the appellate court, not treating the death of the deceased as a mystery, nor giving the accused the mere benefit of a doubt, were of opinion that the circumstances established the man's innocence.

Today, the Code of Criminal Procedure commonly called Criminal Procedure Code (Cr.P.C.) is the main legislation on procedure for administration of substantive criminal law in India. It was enacted in 1973 and came into force on 1 April 1974. It makes a distinction between the judicial confession, those which are made to a judicial magistrate under section 164 of Cr.P.C. or before the court during committal proceeding or during trial and those which are made to any person other than those authorized by law to take confession. It may be made to any person or to police during investigation of an offence.

The confession by Chandra Das in the story was made before a judicial magistrate and hence, a judicial confession. A judicial confession can be relied as proof of guilt against the accused person if it appears to the court to be voluntary and true. A conviction may be based on judicial confession. But, a confession made by an accused person is irrelevant in a criminal proceeding, if the making of the confession appears to the court to have been caused by any inducement, threat or promise having reference to the charge against the accused person. It should not be proceeding from a person in authority. It should also be sufficient, in the opinion of the court, to give the accused person grounds, which would appear to him reasonable, for supporting that by making it he would gain any advantage or avoid any evil of temporal nature in reference to the proceeding against him.

3

Neighbour's Envy

It was a lovely morning when Salman entered Patna. He made way into the village where he was transferred, soaking in the beauty of his new surroundings. As he spotted a small tea shop, he couldn't resist himself from having a steaming cup of *chai* and some snacks.

When he sat down to relish the delicious *samosas*, he saw some men who were noticing him. Perhaps, they were charmed by his western look. Salman gave a welcoming smile to them. As he was sitting alone, he thought of joining them.

When he walked up towards them, they didn't mind him sitting with them.

"So, what do you do, *Saab*?"

"I am a police officer," Salman said humbly.

"Oh! You solve crimes. Then, you must be aware of the Kirpal Singh story right?"

I was perplexed. "Actually, I am new to the city," Salman responded. He was eager to know about this.

"It is a very interesting story, Saab. Everyone knows about him."

As one of the men signalled the *chaiwallah* to refill their cups, Salman was excited to know more about the famous Kirpal Singh story.

•

One fine morning in July 1891, a young bearded gentleman came to a well-known European jeweller's shop. He was handsomely dressed in a long silk coat, white, tight-fitting pyjamas, and wore a smart silk turban. Looking like a Sikh by appearance, he mentioned his name was Kirpal Singh and asked to be shown some jewellery. He introduced himself as the minister in charge of the household of a certain Raja, whose estate was only a few hundred miles away. He was referred by the manager of the jewellery shop to Babu Kahan Chand, the head clerk of the shop, whose duty was to attend to the needs of high-end customers. Kirpal Singh explained to the clerk that he had been specifically instructed by the queen to purchase a large quantity of jewellery as their only daughter was to be married in a few months' time. He spent most of the morning in the shop, examining the whole stock, and made a selection of various valuable articles, amounting in all to about thirty thousand rupees.

Having made his selection, for which an invoice was made, Kirpal Singh asked the manager of the jewellery shop to send Kahan Chand along with him. They would take the jewellery to the Raja's residence so that the queen could make her own selection. Then, they would return what she did not require. The manager assented to this proposal. Kirpal Singh informed that he would like to take the afternoon train back to Raja's estate, to which the manager agreed. The jewellery was packed in two leather bags, and an appointment was made for Kahan Chand to meet Kirpal Singh at the railway station that afternoon.

•

Kahan Chand went to the station accompanied by a bodyguard. Kirpal Singh was already there with a servant. Together, the party boarded the train that evening and arrived at the destination station soon after midnight. On arrival, the minister got out and met a man on the platform, with whom he had some conversation. This conversation seemed to cause Kirpal Singh some perturbation, and he returned to Kahan Chand. With many apologies for the trouble which he had given him, he explained that the queen was making these purchases without the king's knowledge, and that someone had reported the matter to him. So now, if he went on to the Raja's residence with the jewellery, he would get into serious trouble. He said it would be better if Kahan Chand returned home at once with the jewellery. He assured Kahan Chand that it only meant postponing the business for a little while. He was confident of being able to persuade the Raja to agree to the purchase in a few days' time, and when that happened, he would let the firm know and ask them to be good enough to send the jewellery again.

So, Kahan Chand returned to his employer's shop by the next train, together with the bodyguard and the jewels. Kirpal Singh travelled part of the way back with him, and left the train at an intermediate station. Two days later, the manager at the jewellery firm in Patna received the following letter:

> *Dear Sir,*
>
> *I reached home without any trouble. I found no trouble here, for which I am too much obliged. I am sorry for your inconvenience and very ashamed for this. I shall write to you before calling again.*
>
> *Yours faithfully,*
> *Kirpal Singh*

A suspicious mind might have surmised that the manoeuvres of Kirpal Singh were nothing less than a new variety of an old-fashioned confidence trick, carried out with an unusual degree of effrontery, and with a patient optimism rather characteristic of the educated rogue. Four days later, the manager of the firm received a telegram:

"Kindly come through the same train, with scent pots, and other suitable gifts. Will meet you at Kanti"

Kanti was the intermediate station where Kirpal Singh had alighted on the return journey. The goods were packed and Kahan Chand wrapped up the bags in a piece of cloth. He set out again with the same bodyguard. He actually went by a later train, and had to change at a junction, which he reached about midnight. He went off to make enquiries about the train by which he could continue his journey to Kanti. It is not unlikely that he deliberately altered the original itinerary, with the vague notion in his head that if any sort of trick was being played upon him, it would be checkmated by taking this course. But his subsequent conduct showed that if he had really entertained any suspicions about the rendezvous, they were quickly removed.

While he was making his enquiries, his bodyguard saw Kirpal Singh just outside the station waiting room and went to inform his master. Kahan Chand went to meet Kirpal Singh and was greeted by him in the friendliest manner. Kirpal Singh told Kahan Chand that he had sent him another telegram, which had not arrived when Kahan Chand left his employer's shop, making an appointment at the junction. All three men got into the next train and travelled to Kanti, Kahan Chand and Kirpal Singh travelling in the same compartment. They reached Kanti at about three in the morning and left the train. Kirpal Singh proposed that they should at once set out for the Raja's residence, but Kahan Chand demurred, saying that it was too dark.

Kirpal Singh was anxious to get on. He made the rather feeble suggestion that if they waited long, they would have trouble from the sun. Kahan Chand made it clear that he had no intention of proceeding while it was dark. So they waited at the station for some time.

Kahan Chand asked whether any form of conveyance had been provided. Kirpal Singh told him he had a horse for him. Kahan Chand wasn't comfortable riding with three other men walking with him. This was a rather curious objection. It was not clear what he meant by it. It may have been due to modesty, and to a desire not to be treated on a footing different from the rest of the party. It could hardly have been a measure of precaution, as he would have been in a better position in the event of an attack by highwaymen, if he happened to be a good horseman.

The truth was that he was not, and that he had never been on horseback in his life. He would certainly not risk leaving the collection of jewellery in the hands of his bodyguard when he himself was perched on horseback. But, whatever the reason, he definitely declined to be the only member of the party who was to ride. Kirpal Singh then announced that he had arranged for a bullock-cart to meet them on the road. So, it was decided that they should all start off together on foot.

•

There were five of them altogether; Kahan Chand and his bodyguard, Kirpal Singh and his servant, while another man came up just as they were leaving the station, asking to be allowed to accompany them. He was a fellow traveller and Kirpal Singh agreed to it. Daylight was just beginning to appear as they started on their journey. They first passed through the residential quarter of Kanti and emerged on the other side into a jungle.

There appeared to be no metalled road, which seemed to cause Kahan Chand some uneasiness. He asked whether it was the way to the Raja's house. Kirpal Singh replied that it was a short cut. They trudged on for some distance, but Kahan Chand was no more accustomed to walking than he was to riding. Soon, he began to complain of getting tired. Kirpal Singh reassured him by saying that they had not far to go.

They branched off into some fields where there was a good deal of low-growing scrub. Then, Kirpal Singh's servant began to grumble and complained that they were going by a roundabout way. This irked Kirpal Singh, who abused him and told him to hold his tongue. Shortly after this, Kirpal Singh himself said that he was getting tired on which Kahan Chand said, "Surely, Sardar Sahib, you ought not to feel tired. You are a man who is thoroughly accustomed to walking." But Kirpal Singh insisted on sitting down in the scrub and resting.

•

By this time, the sun was well up in the sky , they had been walking for almost two hours, having walked about six miles. Kahan Chand spread a cloth on the ground and he and his bodyguard sat together on it, with the parcel of jewellery on the ground between them. Then, Kirpal Singh and the other two men got up, saying that they wanted water so they went off to procure it. There was no question that Kahan Chand was becoming more and more uneasy. He suggested Kirpal Singh that one of them should stay behind with them, but Kirpal Singh assured him that they were safe while they were in the scrub. After some time, he returned with some water, which the three men drank. Kahan Chand and his bodyguard refused to take any water, possibly fearing that it might have been poisoned.

It is, in fact, remarkable how cautious and full of suspicion Kahan Chand had been for some time. At least, that was the attitude he demonstrated. Yet, he seems to have drifted, in a helpless sort of way, into the ambush which was awaiting him. If he had really entertained his suspicions and fears, there were several things which he might have done without meeting with any effective opposition from Kirpal Singh. He could have refused to leave the station without either a conveyance or some accredited escort. He would probably have avoided the fate in store for him if he had secured some identification of Kirpal Singh from the station officials, or if he had returned to the village when the strange traveller joined them, and Kahan Chand found that he and his bodyguard were in a minority, a situation not to be desired.

•

Having finished his drink of water, Kirpal Singh stood up and began to gaze round, searching the horizon in every direction. Kahan Chand's suspicions were aroused by this conduct, and he asked Kirpal Singh what he was looking for. Kirpal Singh's reply was a strange one. He said he was looking in the direction of a nearby village, in the hope that they would find camels there, which would enable them to continue their journey. The suggestion did not fit well with the plan of the bullock-cart, to which no further reference was made. However, all of them rose to their feet and started off again.

Kahan Chand suddenly heard a noise behind – the crack of *lathis*. He was leading the way with Kirpal Singh. Behind him was his bodyguard carrying two bags of jewellery, followed by the man who had joined them at the station, and then Kirpal Singh's servant. Kahan Chand looked round and saw that his bodyguard had been felled to the ground by the other two men. He had been attacked on the head and was bleeding profusely. It was afterwards discovered that his right arm had been broken by the blows rained upon him. Kahan Chand said to Kirpal Singh, "Sardar Sahib, what is happening?"

The answer he got was, "If you don't keep quiet, you will receive the same treatment yourself."

Kirpal Singh then called out to the other two, "Catch hold of him!"

And then, he proceeded to treat him as a highway robber would treat a defenceless gentleman. He searched through Kahan Chand's pockets, taking everything he could find in them. Kahan Chand tried the effect of further diplomatic negotiations. He said that if Kirpal Singh would leave him the bags which he had brought with him, he could take everything which he had in his pockets. After which, Kirpal Singh returned the contents he had taken from Kahan Chand's pockets. They were probably worth little when compared to thirty thousand rupees worth of jewellery.

The next step was to tie Kahan Chand's hands and feet. This was a simple matter. Kahan Chand then gave himself up for lost, and made his last dying request, that he should not be left in the jungle, but placed somewhere on the road where, if he were lucky, someone would find his dead body.

Though the ears of Kirpal Singh were deaf to these supplications, murder was not a part of his scheme. He again assured Kahan Chand that he would be treated like a gentleman. He went on to assure him that he had no enmity against fellow Indians, but only against the English, though how this was to be satisfied he did not explain. Probably he was thinking of the jewellery, which was almost certainly insured with an English firm. As soon as the other two men, having securely tied the bodyguard, got away with the bags of jewellery, Kirpal Singh untied Kahan Chand's hands, and disappeared with his confederates into the jungle. Kahan Chand released the bodyguard from his bonds, and the two wandered about, trying to find some local place of habitation. They did not know where they were, and the whole country was a broad expanse of jungle and sand. Eventually, they reached a village where there was a railway station. Kahan Chand had been left in possession of his gold watch and his cash, so that he was able to pay for his journey back to Patna.

•

The station master procured them food and water, and attended to the injured bodyguard, who was still bleeding. Kahan Chand then discovered, for the first time, that he was not in British India, but in a native place named Jaynagar State. The station master informed him that there was a head constable belonging to the police force of Jaynagar State in the neighbourhood. At Kahan Chand's request, the constable was sent for and a tonga was procured. Kahan Chand, the bodyguard and the head constable then arranged back to Kanti where they met Hazura Singh, the Superintendent of Police (SP).

To him, Kahan Chand made a formal report of the robbery, and Hazura Singh at once took the matter up. His first business was to find out where the incident had occurred. He sent Kahan Chand off with Sub-Inspector (SI) Fazul-ul-Rahman, who happened to be the Station House Officer (SHO) in charge of the Kanti police station. They went on camels, but they were unable to find the exact spot. Next day, they rode off again on the same quest, this time accompanied by the SP and Kahan Chand's bodyguard.

The SP helped them recall various landmarks to identify the road by which they had travelled to the railway station after being robbed. In this way, they reached the place in the jungle where they had been attacked, and the SP convinced himself that the crime had indeed been committed in the state of Jaynagar so it was his duty to take over the official investigation.

It was important for him to fix the exact locality of the crime because it was close to the frontier of the state, which at this point was bordered by another native state, Rupnagar. It so happened that the respective governments of the two states were not on the best of terms which is why difficulties of jurisdiction and of extradition were apt to arise.

SI Fazul-ul Rahman found the clerk who had despatched the telegram, dated 31 July, which had summoned Kahan Chand to make his second trip with the jewellery. He obtained a general description of the man who had asked for the telegram to be sent. Fazul-ul Rahman was acquainted with more than one bad character who seemed to match the description. Amongst the names mentioned to him was Bir Singh, who seemed suspicious enough to Fazul-ul-Rahman. So, he decided to find out more about him.

Bir Singh was said to be fluent in the use of the English language. He was regarded as a man of some intelligence who was often seen wandering around various railway stations. It was said that he would either try to travel without a ticket or travel by a class superior to that for which he had paid. He was believed to have been a professional photographer once, currently in the employment of the government in Rupnagar.

It was on 5 August that Fazul-ul-Rahman reported to the SP that he had received information which pointed towards Bir Singh. He also managed to find an assistant station master who had recently been at Kanti, but who had just been transferred to another place. From this official, Fazul-ul-Rahman obtained the important information that Bir Singh, whom he knew well, had been at the railway station at Kanti in the early morning when the train brought Kahan Chand and his bodyguard there. This day was 1 August, the actual day of the crime.

Two or three days after receiving this information, Fazul-ul-Rahman went to Rupnagar to visit a friend and learned that Bir Singh was to be found at the house of Jai Ram. Fazul-ul-Rahman stayed with his friend at Rupnagar for the night. By using one of those smart pieces of work at which the Indian police have always been good at, he managed to arrange that his friend should bring Bir Singh to the house in the morning to have a chat. Fazul-ul-Rahman was in *mufti*, his civil dress and not the uniform. His friend talked with Bir Singh on various subjects. As Fazul-ul-Rahman subsequently said, "I did not talk to Bir Singh. I observed him."

This information made a great impression upon SP Hazura Singh. He had already persuaded himself that such a daring robbery must have been committed by a man with brains. It now appeared that the suspected person was in the employment of Rupnagar state. It began to dawn upon the Superintendent that there might be some influence at work behind the commission of the crime and some purpose aimed at beyond the mere robbery of jewellery. He gave certain instructions to another SI, named Tara Singh, and sent him on a mission independent of that entrusted to Fazul-ul-Rahman, and provided him with a head constable named Zafar Husain. It was their job to take Kahan Chand with them to Rupnagar. The SP evidently decided that it was no good giving this duty to Fazul-ul-Rahman, who had become known to Bir Singh now. It should be noted that, up to this moment, the

Superintendent of Jaynagar had not sought the assistance of, nor even communicated with, the police at Rupnagar.

•

On 9 August, Hazura Singh had an interview with Tara Singh and Kahan Chand, and was informed that they had been unable to find Bir Singh in the company of Kahan Chand. It was fairly evident that by this time. Bir Singh and his friends were on their guard. Moreover, the assistant station master from Kanti was also transferred in the meantime, something which may have been no more than a coincidence. But the statement which he made to Fazul-ul-Rahman looked as though his account could not be entirely relied upon. It was conceivable that he was not saying all that he knew. He had been in charge of Kanti during the night when Kahan Chand arrived there. Indeed, he had said that it was at the request of Kahan Chand that he had unlocked the waiting room, to enable him to stay there with his bags until daylight, in this respect agreeing with Kahan Chand's story. But he said that he saw Kirpal Singh on the platform before the arrival of the train. This seemed hardly possible.

Kahan Chand and his bodyguard were both very clear on the point that they had met Kirpal Singh at the junction waiting room at midnight and then, they had all travelled together to Kanti. On this point, they could not have been mistaken as they had no motive for altering the true story. On the other hand, it was difficult to see how the assistant station master could have been mistaken in his recollection of the composition of a small party arriving by train in the small hours of the morning, if he remembered the incident at all.

The assistant station master had been employed at the principal station of Rupnagar, and it is possible that, while he was not prepared to deny that he had seen Bir Singh, about whom such pressing enquiries were being made, he preferred not to say all that he knew. After Tara Singh failed to get in touch with Bir Singh for the purpose of identification by Kahan Chand, the SP came to the conclusion that not much good could be expected from Rupnagar, where they were not likely to receive assistance from the police. So, he sent Tara Singh and Kahan Chand back to Kanti, with instructions to try and get hold of a photograph of Bir Singh, if possible. The same instructions were given to all the police officials were working on the case.

•

Tara Singh's efforts to obtain some relevant information took him to Rupnagar on 14 August. He had two men with him, who were evidently police spies. They took him to the house of a clerk employed in one of the departments of Rupnagar state, who was also one of the official photographers. Tara Singh happened to know a fellow villager who was also in the employment of the state. He was known in the village as Tara Singh's nephew, as is so often the case in villages, being in fact no relation at all, but only a caste fellow.

Tara Singh's nephew suddenly became a person of great importance. Being employed by the state, he was able to get in touch with Bir Singh, who was similarly employed. As Tara Singh naively remarked, when afterwards giving an account of his efforts, "On each occasion that I saw Bir Singh, he was in company with my so-called nephew who told me Bir Singh's name and who he was".

Tara Singh was close to discovering a photograph of Bir Singh. The clerk and official photographer showed Tara Singh and his friends various interesting state photographs, including a group in which Bir Singh appeared. But all Tara Singh's efforts to obtain a temporary possession of this photograph failed, as the clerk said that he was a state photographer, and was not allowed to share copies of such photographs. So, Tara Singh returned to Kanti on the night of 15 August.

Abdul Aziz had been in the police force of Jaynagar for twenty-five years, and was attached to the Criminal Investigation Department (CID). He had some knowledge of men and matters in Rupnagar. On 11 August, the SP employed him to enquire into the robbery case. He was told that Bir Singh was suspected, but there were also others, including two men who were under observation, though it finally turned out that they had nothing to do with the crime. Abdul went to Rupnagar, where he had friends, and made a few secret and discreet enquiries. He happened to get in touch with the kotwal or principal police officer at Rupnagar, and learned from him, in some remarkable way, that he knew that Bir Singh either had, or was supposed to have committed the robbery. The kotwal tried to find out from Abdul Aziz what he was doing in Rupnagar, but Abdul Aziz did not tell him. Abdul Aziz learned about the photograph which had been shown to Tara Singh, and soon discovered where a copy of this photograph was to be found in Jaynagar. He summoned the possessor of it to the kotwali and eventually succeeded in making him hand it over. He then showed it to Kahan Chand, who recognised the features of a man in the group as being those of Kirpal Singh.

•

From this date, the identity of Kirpal Singh with Bir Singh was established. The next question was how to execute the arrest of Bir Singh. It would be dangerous and extremely difficult to catch him in Rupnagar. On 20 August, Abdul Aziz was able to hand over the photograph to Hazura Singh. He assured him that it included the portrait of Bir Singh, whom Kahan Chand had picked out as being Kirpal Singh. The SP then, took the photograph to the shop from which the stolen jewels had come, and obtained further identification of Bir Singh as the supposed Raja's minister who had come there.

Hazura Singh realised that he was in for a contest over the arrest of Bir Singh with the police, and probably also with the state officials of Rupnagar. So he consulted the Prime Minister in his own state of Jaynagar. It came to his knowledge towards the end of August that Bir Singh was in a hill station in British India. So, took steps to procure extradition warrants to enable him to take Bir Singh to Jaynagar if he should succeed in laying hands upon him. But unfortunately, by the time the extradition warrants had been obtained, Bir Singh had left the station.

•

On 8 September, Abdul Aziz went to Rupnagar in plain clothes, taking with him an orderly by the name of Ali Sher Khan. They reached Rupnagar in the evening and Abdul Aziz sent off his orderly to find a man named Teja Singh while he himself remained at the *serai*[1]. Teja Singh used to work as a petition-writer at a place in Abdul Aziz's police station. Abdul Aziz had done him a favour some time back, which helped Teja Singh stay out of jail for an intrigue with a married woman.

Ali Sher Khan found Teja Singh in Rupnagar at the address given to him. Teja Singh told him to go back to his master and inform him that he would follow on. He did not intend to

1. large open waiting place, provided outside big railway stations for the use of travellers

accompany the orderly, though, the latter was in plain clothes. It was just as well that he did not go with him because a group of Rupnagar police stopped the orderly and asked him who he was. He gave some pretext and was not interrogated further. Teja Singh followed on and arrived at the serai.

•

During the meeting at the serai, Teja Singh promised to help Abdul Aziz in his efforts to arrest Bir Singh. Teja Singh said that the best person to make enquiries as to the whereabouts of Bir Singh was Balwant Kuwar, his wife. Abdul Aziz immediately sent Ali Sher Khan to bring her along with him.

The next day, Ali Sher Khan arrived by train with Balwant Kuwar. Abdul Aziz went to the station to meet them. It so happened that the kotwal of Rupnagar was also at the station, so Abdul Aziz held no communication with his friends there and they came with him to the serai. There, Balwant Kuwar was instructed to watch certain houses, and to ascertain where Bir Singh might be found. As she left the serai, the kotwal of Rupnagar left the station on his bicycle, and at around 300 yards from the station, overtook her and spoke to her. If Abdul Aziz had any notion that the police in Rupnagar were watching him, this ought to have put him particularly on his guard, and have warned him that there was danger in trusting Teja Singh and Balwant Kuwar.

But instead, Abdul Aziz decided to disregard the incident. Later that night, they all met in the jungle and Abdul Aziz was informed that Bir Singh had gone away, probably to a place called Champaran. Teja Singh and Balwant Kuwar were asked to immediately go to Champaran and make their enquiries. Abdul Aziz left Rupnagar that night and sent a constable named Fateh

Mahomed with them with instructions that he was to do as they wished. After a few days of untiring effort at Champaran, the trio learnt that Bir Singh was in Delhi. Teja Singh had a married daughter living in Delhi and the suggestion was that Bir Singh might be decoyed there. It was considered advisable that Teja Singh himself should not go to Delhi but Balwant Kuwar accompanied by Abdul Aziz and Ali Sher Khan went to Delhi, and went to the house of Teja Singh's son-in-law SP Hazura Singh also went to Delhi on his own.

•

The next day, Ali Sher Khan was informed by Balwant Kuwar that a party consisting of a man named Daulat Ram, a woman, and a Sikh whose name she could not find out but whose appearance seemed to match with that of Bir Singh. They had been staying at the premises occupied by Teja Singh's son-in-law, but had left there three or four days earlier. The pursuit of Bir Singh began to look like a wild goose chase, and it was open to question whether Teja Singh and Balwant Kuwar were worthy of their trust.

The next plan was that Balwant Kuwar and Ali Sher Khan should return to Rupnagar from Delhi, and that Teja Singh should come to Jaynagar with Abdul Aziz. Back at Jaynagar, Abdul Aziz told Teja Singh in clear terms that he suspected his loyalty. Teja Singh told Abdul Aziz that he did not know where Daulat Ram and Bir Singh had gone to, but he did not think it was any good continuing to trace them at Delhi. Their visit to Delhi was probably for the purpose of disposing of the jewels. He thought that the men they sought had probably returned to Rupnagar. It would be best for Teja Singh, to go back there and send a telegram if there was any news worth communicating. He further added that he knew a woman in Rupnagar who would probably be able to help them to effect the arrest.

On 20 September, Abdul Aziz received a message from Teja Singh:

"The work is ready; come immediately."

Abdul Aziz took his necessary luggage with him and went off to Rupnagar where he went directly to the residence of Teja Singh. Teja Singh informed him that the woman, of whom he had already spoken to him, was there. She had ascertained that the friends of Bir Singh, thinking that the chase was getting rather too hot, had arranged to have him stay in disguise in a military station in British India, and that the woman would be able to attach herself to him which she was quite ready to do. On the journey there, she would arrange that Bir Singh be arrested. Teja Singh added, however, that the woman would want a good deal of money for taking all the trouble.

Abdul Aziz was convinced with this arrangement. It really does seem remarkable that Abdul Aziz had not begun to suspect something by that time. At each stage which he reached under the guidance of Teja Singh, he was told that it was necessary to take a fresh step and he seemed to be getting no nearer to his goal. This was the second woman who had been introduced as an agent-provocateur and it is a rare occurrence in police investigations in those days to utilise the services of women at all. He was required to find, or at least promise, a substantial sum of money. Nonetheless, Abdul Aziz continued to nibble. Whether he hoped to acquire kudos from his principals, however feeble the results he was able to show, or whether he firmly believed in the friendship of Teja Singh and his gratitude for past services rendered, or whether he hoped to obtain sound information for himself, and trusted his own wits to be able to profit from it, he continued to nibble.

Teja Singh went on to say that the woman actually wanted no less than one thousand rupees, and that, if that amount were promised, he would arrange an interview between her and Abdul Aziz.

On the matter of pay, Abdul Aziz reasoned out with himself, and explained it to Teja Singh. The firm of jewellers had offered a reward of fifteen hundred rupees for the recovery of the lost property, and the state of Jaynagar would be certain to give another if Bir Singh were captured. As the arrest was imminent, he could afford to discount some of his promised gains, and agree to pay the woman one thousand. One can only say, from one's experience of the police in India that in all likelihood, Abdul Aziz had not the slightest intention of ever doing anything of that kind. He must have trusted his intelligence, or his good fortune, to find a way out of paying anyone, particularly a woman, such an extortionate sum. But he promised to pay it, and Teja Singh left him. He returned an hour later with the woman. She kept her face covered, but Abdul Aziz was able to recognise both her general appearance and her voice. Her name was Khairan.

Khairan detailed the arrangements she was ready to make for her journey, not merely with Bir Singh, but even with the stolen jewels – a contingency so extravagant and extraordinary that it ought to have put Abdul Aziz on his guard once again. She told him that she would let him know at what railway station he would find them. There must have been something about Abdul Aziz which infused these people with confidence.

Then, Teja Singh whispered to Abdul Aziz that the woman was very fond of money. He added that she would probably like something on account. This was both probable and natural.

Abdul Aziz had in his pocket two notes of fifty rupees each, being government money with which he had been provided by Hazura Singh for unforeseen contingencies, or what the French call *imprevuei*. Khairan was certainly an imprevuei, and he gave her one of the notes. Teja Singh and Khairan then, left on their return journey to Rupnagar, after making an appointment with Abdul Aziz at a spot in the jungle near the railway station at Rupnagar. Before going to this appointment, Abdul Aziz had an interview with Hazura Singh, to whom he narrated what had happened. Hazura Singh gave him instructions to go to Rupnagar and keep the appointment, but to return by the early morning train.

•

Abdul Aziz took Ali Sher Khan with him. On their arrival at Rupnagar, they had another fine goose-chase in their unavailing efforts to find Teja Singh at the appointed place. Abdul Aziz took the most elaborate precautions. Ali Sher Khan got out on the platform with instructions to look for Teja Singh in the station and in the passenger-shed. Meanwhile, Abdul Aziz got out on to the line, on the other side. This was such a frequent method of alighting for the casual traveller that he would attract no attention. By wandering on the line, he would probably be taken for an ordinary foot-passenger who had lost his way and was looking for the passenger-shed, where it is the commonest thing in the world for hordes of third-class passengers to remain for twenty-four hours, frequently sleeping on the cooler and quieter platform until it suited them to get into a train. He walked to the appointed place in the jungle, but found nobody there.

Ali Sher Khan had taken the luggage with him. This consisted of the carefully coded parcel, a small amount of bedding, a *lota* or water-jug, a metal tumbler, a *huqqa* and a small change of clothing, all of which Abdul Aziz had brought with him, when he did not know whether he might have to stay a night or two at Rupnagar. Ali Sher Khan failed to find Teja Singh so he went off in search of Abdul Aziz, carrying the bundle of luggage with him. They met at the gateman's cabin, close to the level-crossing. Lying outside was the usual *charpoy*, or string cot, where the gateman slept in the open, trusting to luck or to habit to wake up when he is needed for the performance of his duty. On this charpoy Ali Sher Khan deposited the luggage and leaving Abdul Aziz there, went off into the city to Teja Singh's house. There, he found Balwant Kuwar, who was alone, and who told him that Teja Singh had gone to the station to meet Abdul Aziz. So, Ali Sher Khan returned and re-joined Abdul Aziz.

•

The train had arrived at about 6:00 p.m., but by this time it had become dark. Thinking that he had possibly missed Teja Singh, Abdul Aziz sent Ali Sher Khan back to the house to see if Teja Singh had returned. Ali Sher Khan was then told by Balwant Kuwar that Teja Singh had come in, in the meanwhile, and had gone out again. He had better tell Abdul Aziz to come straight to the house. So, Ali Sher Khan returned to the level-crossing a second time, and gave Abdul Aziz Balwant Kuwar's message. Thereupon, they both went off to Teja Singh's house, carrying the luggage with them. Abdul Aziz was getting anxious as to how he would be able to carry out the Superintendent's order to return by the early morning train. The train left at 1 a.m., and it was now getting on for 8:00 p.m. It was the rule in Rupnagar for the city gates to be closed at 10:00 p.m., and unless travellers got away before that hour, they had to spend the night there. But Ali Sher Khan assured him that if they had any difficulty in getting through the gates after ten 10:00 p.m., he knew places in the city walls where they could get through.

In the courtyard of Teja Singh's house, they found Balwant Kuwar cooking food and two men, who appeared to be Sikh cultivators, sitting there. Teja Singh was sitting on the roof with another man. Balwant called out to Teja Singh that the Pundit had come. Abdul Aziz and Ali Sher Khan went up to the roof, the latter still carrying the luggage. Teja Singh proposed that they should eat before talking, and Abdul Aziz, nothing loth, agreed. Partly on the account of hot weather, and partly because he did not wish to attract attention to any kind of police uniform, Abdul Aziz had changed his trousers for a *dhoti*. He appeared to have been comfortable and unsuspecting, quite willing to await the convenience of Teja Singh.

After the meal was over, Abdul Aziz reproached Teja Singh for not having kept his appointment. Teja Singh replied that he had been to the station, but had failed to find him. He then went on: "The woman's husband is ill and though Bir Singh is ready to start, she is making excuses in order to detain him, so that she can give you information before they set out. You will understand better when you have talked with her. I had better go and see her."

Then, Teja Singh left. He returned in half an hour, saying that the woman was alone in her house and wanted Abdul Aziz to go and talk to her. Abdul Aziz did not like this suggestion. He pointed out that he might be seen and that the plot would be ruined. However, Teja Singh assured him that there was no risk as the woman's husband was in hospital and she was alone, so that no one would be likely to see. Abdul Aziz was still anxious about getting out before 10:00 p.m. and catching his train back. So, he decided to get on with the job, and, leaving Ali Sher Khan at the house with the luggage, he went off with Teja Singh, who took him to Khairan's house. Teja Singh went in first, while Abdul Aziz remained outside. In a few minutes Teja Singh called him in.

There was no one there. The room was dark, but a lantern was hanging on the wall. Abdul Aziz asked, 'Where are they?'

Teja Singh replied, "I left her here. She must be somewhere nearby. Sit down while I go and look for her."

So, Abdul Aziz sat down on the charpoy, which was in the room near the entrance and waited. He had not sat there for many minutes before he heard a sound as of men's footsteps drawing near from the street outside. He turned and saw a body of men making towards the door of the house. He could not fail to notice, from the sound made by their footsteps, that some of them were wearing shoes. It flashed across his mind that there must be police officers amongst them, and that he had been led into a trap. He had hardly time to rise from his seat and to face his visitors before ten or twelve men in police uniform rushed upon him and, seizing hold of him, flung him, with incredible violence, back upon the charpoy and proceeded to bind his hands and legs with stout cords.

Of course, neither he nor Ali Sher Khan were able to catch their train; and when the Superintendent met a train arriving later in the day, in the hope that they might come by it, he learned from the railway police that one of his darogas had been arrested in Rupnagar on a charge of rape. The principal complainant was a young woman of about twenty years of age, named Rahmat-un-Nissa. She was the wife of Inayat Mohamed, a Sheikh, who lived in Delhi. She did not get on well with her husband, who did not live regularly with her, but visited her from time to time at the house where Khairan lived at Rupnagar and cohabited with her. She complained of his cruelty, particularly in relation to the sexual act. Khairan was the sister of Inayat Mohamed. She was married to Mohamed Ibrahim and Mohamed Ibrahim, Khairan, and

Rahmat-un-Nissa all lived together in a house a few paces down a lane which led into a main street. The house being recognised as one of ill-fame, the two women had the reputation of being of loose character. The allegation that Abdul Aziz had asked his way to the house, and had made no secret of his intention to visit a woman there, whether true or untrue, caused no surprise amongst the people living in the neighbourhood. Both Inayat Mohamed and Mohamed Ibrahim had been connected with some kind of police force at one time or another.

•

Rahmat-un-Nissa later, during trial, conceded that a statement formerly made by her was untrue. She adopted the usual feminine resort of attributing her previous falsehood to the compulsion of her husband. She declared that she no longer desired to live with him. She went on to say that she was wandering about on the platform when she met her future husband, Inayat Mohamed, and he asked her to marry him. She said that she would. Inayat Mohamed gave another account of it, but not always the same one.

She was examined by a magistrate at her own house and she had this to say:

> "One night, at seven or 7 p.m. or 8 p.m., I was sleeping on a charpoy in the outer room. Khairan woke me up, saying 'Get up; you are asleep with your face uncovered. There are men here.' I woke up and saw two men standing in the courtyard. I sat on a small stool in the inner room. The two men came in and sat in the outer room. Abdul Aziz sat on a charpoy. He asked Khairan where Mohamed Ibrahim had gone. She said he had gone out to some *tamasha* and would not be back for two or three

hours. Khairan then, filled a huqqa for Abdul Aziz, and he began to smoke and asked for some betels and gave Khairan some pice to go out and get some. Khairan said she would not take his money, but would go and purchase some with her own.

As soon as she went out, Abdul Aziz began to make jokes to me. I asked him what right he had to do this. As he did not stop, I went into an inner room where he could not see me. The other man went outside and closed the door. Abdul Aziz then came to me, and putting his hand on my mouth, forced my head back. I tried to call out, saying that he was dishonouring me. He began to pull the upper part of my clothes down and expose my breasts and bit me once on each check. I shouted for help and struggled. While we were struggling together, I bit him twice on the chest. My clothes got torn. He opened the string of my pyjamas and pulled them down as far as my ankles. He then undid his dhoti. He took hold of my legs and put one of my feet on each shoulder. While he held me in this way, he got on his knees, and proceeded to have connection with me. He had put out the lamp in the outer room but my cries must have been heard, as two men came in to my assistance. It was only when they arrived that he got off me. He tried to run away, but the two men caught hold of him, and held him. I was weeping. After a long while Khairan came back and I told her what had happened. She went off to make a report. Meanwhile, some more men from the neighbourhood came in and later on, the police arrived, and the kotwal had Abdul Aziz, handcuffed. He took away some things from the charpoy where I had been lying and he round some broken glass bangles. Sometime after the police had gone away with Abdul Aziz, a dai (native nurse or midwife) came and examined me and my clothes. She examined me again the next day. I had suffered pain and inflammation."

Khairan, who gave her age as 35, made a statement to the Magistrate to the following effect:

"I knew Abdul Aziz as he was said to be related in some way to my husband's family. He had been to our house and I had cooked for him, but had not spoken to him. I used to preserve purdah (the veil) before him. Rahmat-un-Nissa also always preserved purdah. On this occasion my husband was out, although he had been ill. Abdul Aziz came to our house with another young man about 9:00 p.m. The other man appeared to be a servant and carried a bundle and some clothing. We were both lying asleep on charpoys in the outer room. The doors into the courtyard were closed but were not chained. The door was pushed open, and I woke up.

Abdul Aziz called "Ibrahim".

I asked, "Who is there?"

He said, "It is me, Abdul Aziz".

I said to him, "Stop a minute! The girl is sleeping with her face uncovered".

I woke Rahmat-un-Nissa, and she sat on a stool between the two rooms. The second man sat on the ground. Abdul Aziz sat on a charpoy and I prepared a huqqa for him. He said he would wait till Ibrahim came home. He asked me to get some betel and offered me some pice, but

I said I would get it with my own money, and went out to buy it. I was away for about half an hour as all the shops were shut. When I came back, Abdul Aziz was being held in the outer room by two men. Rahmat-un-Nissa was standing in the inner room. Her breasts were exposed, and her pyjamas were stained and she was crying. She had marks of bites on her cheeks, which were bleeding. Her glass bangles had been broken. She said to me, 'This man has deprived me of my honour, and raped me'.

I said to Abdul Aziz, 'Why have you done such an evil thing?' I told the two men to hold him while I fetched the kotwal. I went to the kotwal's house, expecting to find him there, but by chance I met him, on my way, in the grass market, and told him what had happened. He sent a constable with me to the kotwali, where I made a report. I did not send the servant of Abdul Aziz to buy the betel because he did not know the way."

•

Witnesses from the *mohalla* or immediate neighbourhood were called to corroborate the stories told by these two women. Chief, of course, among these witnesses were the two men who came in first on hearing the cries of Rahmat-un-Nissa. Strictly speaking, from the point of view of the law, no such corroboration was really essential. If corroboration were required, it was to be found in amplitude in the flesh marks, fresh and blood-stained, on the bodies of the woman and the man, and in the weeping condition of the woman, and her stained clothing and broken bangles. Misunderstanding sometimes arises about the meaning of corroboration, and the difference between mere technical corroboration, on the one hand, and the weight to be attached, on the other, to evidence which is put forward in support of such a story. If the appearances just mentioned, found on the spot, were really there, they were in themselves ample corroboration.

The culprit, in fact, was caught practically red-handed. It is unnecessary to examine in detail the evidence of these corroborating witnesses. It contained many inconsistencies. But it contained also certain a priori improbability, which would have made it almost certain that an English jury, trying the case, would have refused to act upon their evidence.

One difficult feature about it was the reason they gave for having entered the house at all. They said they were attracted by the sounds of a woman's voice, apparently crying, or in some distress. But it can hardly be said to be the usual practice, or a natural proceeding, for anyone passing along a street, and hearing a voice crying inside a house, to enter, as a matter of course, in the expectation of discovering someone within in the act of committing a crime.

But an even more glaring difficulty was the story they told about a second man, who was Ali Sher Khan, who, according to the woman, was waiting outside, but who, according to the neighbours, rushed out on their approach. Why they made no effort to catch hold of him, or to follow him, but assumed, one and all, that the disturbance was due to someone else inside, so that they all went in and ignored the man escaping, no one attempted to explain.

•

There were also difficulties in accepting the explanation of the arrival of the large police force, after Khairan had left the house a second time, when she learned what had happened, and had found the kotwal in the grass market. She had said that the kotwal had sent her off with a constable to the kotwali to make a report. It did not appear, under these circumstances, how the kotwal knew where to go to find the culprit, and why he took so many policemen with him. Someone may have known Khairan's house, but she did not say who she was, and she said she had her face covered. The kotwal's explanation about the number of police whom he was so conveniently able to take with him to the house was, to say the least of it, quite remarkable. There were some public festivities going on, and an unusual force of police was out in the streets that night. But, according to the kotwal it so happened that, when Khairan found him at the grass market, he had gathered a number of constables there in order to detail them for their night duties, and he took them with him to the house, so that he might complete the business of drafting them off to their duties, when he had finished enquiring into the affair at Khairan's house.

At this stage, it is natural to ask oneself what probability there is, on general grounds, of the story of a rape having been committed by Abdul Aziz, under the special circumstances in which he was placed, having a grain of truth in it at all. He was in Rupnagar on a very special and responsible mission, for the arrest of Bir Singh. Having regard to the relations between the police force to which he himself belonged, and that of Rupnagar, he was, so to speak, in an enemy's country. He was there, more or less in disguise. His mission was a secret one, for which he had employed, as he thought, a friend as a sort of spy. He was engaged in a plot which required both secrecy and expedition. He was in close contact with his superior officer, and under orders to get away by the night train. He had his personal luggage and another member of his own force with him.

Under these circumstances, when for all he knew he was being watched, is it conceivable that he would have been so mad as to court disaster either by going into a house of ill-fame, if it was one, or of attempting an outrageous rape upon a perfectly respectable woman. Such conduct becomes still more difficult to believe when it is remembered that it was alleged to have been committed in the very house to which he had been directed for the completion, as he hoped and trusted, of his mission. These considerations seem insuperable.

•

Abdul Aziz recognised the leader of the police party that arrested him as the Court Inspector. They carried him off the charpoy where he had been sitting, and, taking him into the inner room, threw him upon the charpoy there. Someone took hold of his beard and shook his head from side to side, a pleasing method of breaking down his resistance. The Inspector, according to Abdul Aziz, slapped his face with his open hand, and indulged in the favourite abuse of indecent references to his mother and his sister. They took off his coat, tore his clothes, and bit him twice on his naked chest. They pulled down his dhoti and two men scratched his thighs, till the blood came, and then left his lower parts naked. Teja Singh was in the attack, and he searched Abdul Aziz' pockets, and found the other fifty-rupee note, which he had notgiven to the woman at the interview. This was taken from him, together with his diary and notebook and his watch. They then carried him into the outer room, and put him on the charpoy there.

The kotwal then arrived, with some more constables and handcuffs. He was carrying a revolver and one of the constables had a breech-loading gun and some cartridges. Abdul Aziz was then handcuffed. The kotwal gave an order, "Bring them!"

The two women, Khairan and Rahmat-un Nissa, were brought in. The lantern was still burning on the wall, and Abdul

Aziz was able to recognise the women's faces. Rahmat-un-Nissa stood by the foot of the charpoy. On the order of the kotwal the upper part of her dress was disarranged by some constables, and her breasts were exposed. Abdul Aziz complained that he was himself exposed, so they covered up his legs with his dhoti. They told the woman to have a good look at him, and then an order was given for the neighbours to be brought in. The women were sent out into the courtyard, and Abdul Aziz was taken back to the inner room. After a few minutes some neighbours came in with the police, and to them the charge was made by the police that Abdul Aziz had been found raping Rahmat-un-Nissa. They were taken into the inner room, and there Abdul Aziz and Rahmat-un-Nissa were shown to them. It was at this point that Abdul Aziz noticed that the woman had a bloodstained mark on each cheek, which looked as though they might be bites, and he asserted positively that these had not been there when he first saw her, and that they had been made while he was handcuffed and in the hands of the constables.

As a piece of realism, this conduct on the part of the constables in biting or scratching the checks of the unfortunate woman, who must have been almost as disgusted by the treatment inflicted upon her as Abdul Aziz himself, has the distinct merit of originality and realism. It showed, however, great poverty of imagination. No doubt the idea was to aggravate the offence as much as possible, though the offence was one so aggravated in itself, that the addition of a small detail of this kind could have little effect upon the mind of any ordinary person who had to adjudicate upon the case, the judge or the jury.

What it did, however, was to throw great doubt upon the truth of the story of the rape. If one considers the story as told by the woman herself, one finds great difficulty in believing that any man, however drunk or mad with lust he might be, would attempt such a useless and difficult form of cruelty. It would certainly very much impede his efforts, and he would derive no benefit or satisfaction from such an unpleasing form of attention.

But more than that, it was in the highest degree absurd to suppose that a responsible police officer, pressed for time, and desiring to commit a rape of any kind in such circumstances, would go out of his way to do anything so insane.

In the face of such astounding allegations as were made by Abdul Aziz about his treatment that evening, he was finally taken off through the crowd which had, by this time, gathered on the spot, to the house of the Chief of Police. There, the women were waiting for him, with their faces covered. Khairan had made the charge. She said that she was the wife of Mohamed Ibrahim, a mounted policeman, and that Abdul Aziz was a perfect stranger to her, and that she had never seen him before.

The Chief was alleged by Abdul Aziz to have then said, "Khairan, can't you keep the matter quiet, and take twenty or thirty rupees and say no more about it." Her answer was said to have been, "Sardar Sahib, if he had only had connection with me, it would not have mattered, but I cannot permit the honour of my relative being outraged".

•

After this little comedy had been completed, the women were allowed to go, and the Chief said that the matter must take the usual course. Abdul Aziz then complained to the Chief that he had been led into a trap by Teja Singh – a circumstance which he might well have suspected a long time before, and so saved himself much suffering and humiliation – and that he had come from the house of Teja Singh where his orderly, Ali Sher Khan, and his bedding still were. The Chief then gave orders for the orderly and the bedding to be fetched and said that he would make enquiries of Teja Singh in the morning. So, Abdul Aziz was led off to the lock-up and was eventually placed in the jail where his legs were put into heavy irons, which were chained to the wall. He was subsequently examined, together with his dhoti, by a doctor, and some three or four days later he was taken to the house of Khairan, where a magistrate recorded the statements of the two women in his presence.

According to Ali Sher Khan, when Abdul Aziz left with Teja Singh to go to the woman's house, he went to sleep. He was on the roof, and, as far as he could say, it was about 11:00 p.m. when he was awakened by a man shaking his legs and telling him to get up, because Abdul Aziz and Teja Singh wanted him downstairs. He went down the steps, taking the luggage with him, and as soon as he got into the street he was confronted by a large body of men, who immediately seized hold of him. He was knocked about with sticks and fists, and, on asking why he was being arrested in this way, he was informed that he would find out later on. The luggage fell from his hands and he did not see it again. He was taken to the kotwali and there handcuffed and locked up for the night. He again asked what the charge against him was, and was told, generally, that there were too many "badmashes" (bad elements) coming into the state of Rupnagar to cause trouble.

•

The next day, he was taken before an Inspector and ordered to make a statement to the effect that he had gone, on the last evening, to the house of Mohamed Ibrahim, with Abdul Aziz, and that there, after sending out the wife, Khairan, to buy betel, Abdul Aziz had made him sit outside, and that while he was doing so Abdul Aziz had raped a woman in the house. Ali Sher Khan refused to make this statement. Eventually he did make a rambling sort of statement to the effect required, after he had been submitted to a specimen of what are known as 'Third Degree' methods. The methods employed to extract admissions out of him, as subsequently described by him, are worth repeating. They strike one as original, but not as methods which ought to be treated as precedents for similar occasions.

They first placed him on his face on the ground and beat him, on his bare buttocks, with shoes. There was nothing original about this. But the real effort of undue pressure was yet to come. Ali Sher Khan said that he was made to sit down cross-legged while four or five men stood over him and placing their heels upon the inner surface of his thighs, they forced his thighs up and down with their heels. He cried out with pain, the only effect of which was to cause the constables to redouble their efforts, until the unfortunate man gave way under the strain. He then, made a sort of confession, which was taken down by a member of the police force, whom he believed at the time to be a magistrate. Later on, he was taken before a magistrate to make a formal confession.

The method adopted for taking confession was, according to Ali Sher Khan, original. He was not asked whether any pressure, or inducement, had been used upon him in order to obtain his original admission. Nor was he asked to make any fresh confession or statement to the Magistrate. He was merely asked by the Magistrate whether the statement, which was then on the table before him, was his, which it certainly was, and the Magistrate then proceeded to copy it out. He was then, told to put his thumb impression upon the copy, which he knew better than to refuse to do. This seems to be all the evidence which the police could possibly have made available for the case against him. But it was considered to be sufficient to put Ali Sher Khan upon his trial, and he was committed to the sessions.

•

Although, Ali Sher Khan's part was an entirely subordinate one, it is worthwhile to consider what case there was against him. The charge could only be that of aiding and abetting the rape. But if a subordinate officer has to accompany his superior to a house, and when he gets there, is told to sit outside and wait while his superior goes inside, he is, so far, doing no more than his duty, and is certainly countenancing no crime, nor even an act of trespass. He may have reason to suspect that his superior is up to no good.

But if the door is closed, he cannot possibly know what particular form of iniquity is being either contemplated or perpetrated. Even if it be the case that a man who, knowing that his companion is intending to commit a rape, if he can, remains outside to give warning, 'keeping eye' as one used to say, he may be held guilty of aiding and abetting, this conduct could not be attributed to Ali Sher Khan, who was not alleged to have given any warning of the neighbours' approach, but to have run away when he saw them coming.

The alleged offence was committed on the 21 September. The hearing before the Magistrate opened on the 26 September. The accused were committed to trial on the 28 September. The trial at Sessions began on the 4 October and was finished on 6 October and the judgment recording the convictions and punishments of both accused was given on the 12 October— just twenty-one days after the alleged offence.

Not many courts could match this record. But, the treatment of the prisoner's friends was quite otherwise. The first step taken by the Superintendent of Jaynagar, Hazura Singh, when he learned of the arrest of Abdul Aziz, was, after a flying visit himself to Rupnagar, to depute Hardial Singh, one of his Sub-Inspectors, and two other members of the force, to go there, and to make enquiries with a view to ascertaining the charge. He could not believe that Abdul Aziz could have been guilty of such conduct while engaged upon an official mission of importance, and he realised that it was of little use going himself until he was armed with some state document authorising him to take official action. 'The doom' of Hardial Singh was 'extremely hard'. He also was arrested. He was charged and convicted and sentenced to six months' imprisonment for having been 'drunk and disorderly'.

Judging by what the Chief of Police was alleged by Hazura Singh to have said at an interview which took place between them, one of the grievances against him was that he was a member of the C.I.D., and that he had been taking notes, in court, of the proceedings before the Magistrate. This may have appeared to the Magistrate to have been 'disorderly conduct', but it can hardly have been reasonably regarded as a sign of intoxication. He displayed other symptoms of 'an atmosphere of preparedness' for disorder by taking a rather stronger line than anyone else in his requests to be allowed to interview Abdul Aziz and Ali Sher Khan, and to attend the court proceedings.

And when he was threatened with proceedings against himself for having been guilty of such conduct, he naturally asked what his offence was, and under what provision of the law he could be so charged, he was informed that there was an ordinance which rendered anyone liable to imprisonment for a maximum period of two years, who was found drunk in any public place to which women had access. This enigmatical dictum must have puzzled the Sub-Inspector, and may have been intended to alarm him and to keep him quiet. It was under that ordinance that he was arrested.

But, on the other hand, it became clear to the police of the state of Jaynagar, and to those who were anxious to get into touch with Abdul Aziz, and to watch the case against him, that the Magistrate's court was not a 'public place', in the true sense of the word, for, from this time forward they were refused admission while the case was going on against Abdul Aziz and Ali Sher Khan.

•

Hazura Singh arrived at Rupnagar on the 26 September, having procured from the Foreign Minister of Jaynagar a letter addressed to one of the Ministers in Rupnagar. He was met there by some of his officers who detailed to him their experiences up to date. They were accompanied by some of the relatives of Abdul Aziz, amongst whom was his son. The proceedings on the charge against the two accused had begun that day. They had been to the court, but had been refused admission. They were told that it was the rule of the state that no one could attend the court without having first obtained permission from the High Court. So, they went to the High Court to obtain permission, but although it was only ten o'clock in the morning, they found that the Judges had left. So, they went to the residences of the Judges, and were there told that they must apply at the High Court, during office hours, next day. They then returned to the Magistrate's court, and renewed their application there. The result of this visit was that they were not only refused admission, but were told by the police that if they remained there, they would be arrested. They were not allowed to hire a tonga, and had to walk to the station.

Hazura Singh then went to pay his call on the Minister. He asked that Abdul Aziz should be released on bail, and that his documents should be handed over to the Superintendent. The Minister said that he would communicate with the Chief of Police.

Hazura Singh requested that the Chief should be sent for, but the Minister said that he would not come to his house if he sent for him. Hazura Singh then suggested that the Minister should accompany him in his car to the house of the Chief, but to this the Minister, not unnaturally, objected that it was beneath his dignity to visit the Chief of Police. Hazura Singh then asked what he should do in order to obtain an interview with Abdul Aziz, and to assist him in his defence. The Minister replied that he did not know, as it was outside his department.

Hazura Singh then, drove to the kotwali, and asked to be allowed to enter his arrival in the general diary. He was told to put his application in writing. He thereupon asked if he would be given a receipt for it. He was told that the kotwal could not give him a receipt before consulting the Chief of Police. So, Hazura Singh asked for an interview with the Chief. A man was sent to the house, and brought back the reply that the Chief could see him at 5:00 p.m. Hazura Singh then left the kotwali and went to the house of the Magistrate, who was also the Superintendent of the jail. He explained that all that he wanted was an interview with Abdul Aziz, in order to arrange for his defence. The Magistrate said that this could only be done with the permission of the Chief of Police.

So, at 5:00 p.m., Hazura Singh reached the office of the Chief. The Chief said that he understood that the arrest of Bir Singh was sought, but that the police declined to give him up on account of some cross claim, or grievance, which they had against the police of Jaynagar. With regard to the case of Abdul Aziz, he referred to Khairan as being a woman of the worst character and repeated the whole story about Abdul Aziz as was in police records. He, the Chief, then added that he had offered her twenty rupees to withdraw the case, and that she had said that she would not have complained if the act had been done to her, but that she could not tolerate a relative being outraged. The Chief added that, as the case was now public property, it would have to proceed, and that Hazura Singh would not be allowed to interview Abdul Aziz, or to attend the proceedings in court, and that no outside vakil, or lawyer, would be allowed to be heard. This being all the response he could get to his simple demand, after struggling for the best part of a day, the Superintendent returned to his home in his car and came back next day.

•

On his arrival he found his subordinate officers, about one hundred yards from the court. They reported that the adjourned hearing had begun that morning before sunrise, and that they had tried to attend it, but that, on entering the court, they had been turned out. They had then been to the High Court, but found no Judges there. While the Superintendent was outside the court, a messenger from the court came to him and told him that unless he had the permission of the Chief of Police, he must not loiter outside. Just then he received another message that the Magistrate wished to see him. As he went into the court as Abdul Aziz was being taken out. The Magistrate complained to Hazura Singh that his men were annoying him unlawfully, and that one of them had done something with a piece of stamped paper which rendered him liable to punishment, under a certain ordinance, by imprisonment for two years.

Hazura Singh resorted to a rather smart move, and stated that he would direct the man to surrender and to take his trial. This seems to have acted like the pouring of oil on troubled waters, and the Magistrate said that he would not proceed against the man, as no formal complaint had been made, while the Court Inspector placed himself at the disposal of Hazura Singh. So Hazura Singh asked him if he could arrange for an interview with Abdul Aziz. The Court Inspector said that he had no objection, and that the court could give permission. On the matter being mentioned to the Magistrate, he gave his consent. This seemed to be all that Hazura Singh had been waiting for, or required, and he proceeded to the longed-for interview. But a fresh difficulty arose in the Magistrate's mind. Abdul Aziz was then outside and, on his way, to jail. So, the Magistrate explained that the application had to be in writing. It is true that he might have sent for Abdul Aziz and had him brought back into court, but that does not seem to have occurred to him. He wrote something on an application, which was eventually handed in, and Hazura Singh was compelled to point out that the order was meaningless.

He then, orally requested that he might be allowed to have an interview, then and there, in the presence of the Magistrate himself, without the necessity of following him to jail and going through the formal procedure. The Magistrate said that he could not allow that. Hazura Singh suggested that Abdul Aziz might be brought back into court for the purpose of selecting a lawyer.

The Magistrate then had four *vakils*, or lawyers, produced, but no Abdul Aziz. The Superintendent chose a vakil, and obtained an order for an interview at the jail, where he proceeded in company with the vakil. The door of the jail was not opened to them, but the Superintendent was allowed to put his copy of the order through the window. Having done this, he had to wait some ten or fifteen minutes. The vakil chosen happened, curiously enough, to have been formerly in the police in the state of Jaynagar. During the wait outside, he let himself go. He said that he did not want to appear for the defence. He could do no good because, although it was a fabricated case, everyone was in it, and that if he defended the case properly, he would certainly be ruined. This seemed to cause Hazura Singh no surprise, and he released him from his engagement.

On the jailor's return, the door was again not opened. The jailor told Hazura Singh that he must apply to the High Court, where the petition would be forwarded, with a note by the jailor that he did not think the interview ought to be allowed to take place. As the High Court was not sitting, Hazura Singh appreciated the value of this fresh proposal, and did nothing on it.

As a last resort he went back to the Minister, to whom he had the letter of introduction, and whom he had already seen, and he requested him that the papers of Abdul Aziz should be handed over. The Minister asked to be supplied with a list of them. Hazura Singh pointed out that it was impossible for him to do this unless he had an interview with Abdul Aziz, who alone knew what the papers consisted of. The Minister then, expressed his regret that he could do nothing more, and the Superintendent returned home once again, having affected nothing by his two visits. It so happened that the only friendship and assistance extended to Abdul Aziz during the short time he had to wait before his case was disposed of at Sessions, came from the jailor, whom he had known, in days gone by, in the police force. He advised him to confess, and told him that if he did so he would have a better chance of escaping with his life. Whether he really believed this, and wished to help Abdul Aziz, one cannot say. But Abdul Aziz always said that he felt he was able to turn to him as a friend.

•

When Abdul Aziz was ordered by the court to put in a written statement, which he had to prepare in jail, the jailor told him to show him whatever he wrote. This the prisoner did, and at the instance of the jailor, he omitted and altered several things, which the jailor assured him would only do him harm. It is possible that this was honestly done in Abdul Aziz's interest. Of course, it produced the result that his written statement did not contain all that he subsequently stated as having actually happened to him, and it omitted many important facts. But so far as the trial was concerned, it is unlikely that the contents of the written statement made much difference.

Abdul Aziz – and also the case of Ali Sher Khan – was unrepresented, friendless, and practically defenceless. And realising that nothing was to be gained by anything which he either said or did, he said and did as little as possible, for the moment resigned and patiently hoping that someday a change of fortune would bring redress. He was sentenced to five years' imprisonment and a fine of five hundred rupees, a severe, but not excessive, punishment for a bad case of rape.

Ali Sher Khan received only six months, which looked as though the judge had some doubt about his guilt. There was an appeal to the High Court. But an Appellate Court can do little in a case of this kind, when it has not seen the witnesses and the accused has not called evidence.

4

The Compromise

The case was one in which the question of motive loomed large. The suggestion of a sex intrigue was the main defence. The judge rejected it. The body of the deceased had been brutally mutilated, and his nose, and genitals, alike had been removed. This had but one meaning. The judge held that this had been done by the accused with the intention of throwing suspicion upon other people, presumably the relatives of the guilty woman.

But he overlooked the fact that this laceration of the body was an idle performance as a false scent, unless there were some sex intrigue in which the deceased was involved. There was a great volume of evidence which supported the allegation, and it must be added, to have been established to the satisfaction of most reasonable men. But the motive was actually irrelevant, if the direct evidence was believed. And the judge further overlooked the fact that while he used the topic of motive to differentiate between the two sets of accused, he was really convicting four of them on the strength of the direct evidence which applied, in effect, equally to all.

•

The murdered man, Bhawar Singh, was a prosperous zamindar and cultivator of the village of Semari. About a year before his death, the deceased, or one of his tenants, had caused a certain mud house, in which the tenant had lived, to revert back to his possession. He utilised the ground floor for storing grain and tethering cattle, and he slept, at any rate during the hot weather, on a charpoy, or cot, on the roof. He had two near relatives, his brother, Sripal Singh, and his cousin, Ajgar Singh, who lived in the ancestral house, which Bhawar Singh had deserted, at nights, for the roof of his new granary. He was the mukhia, or headman, of the village. Secondly, the roof of his granary was about twenty paces from the house of Badlu with whose wife he was alleged to have an intrigue. The mukhia's word, up to a point, was law in the village, and it was said that there were occasions when, if he wanted a young and attractive woman brought to his residence at night, she is brought. That could only happen when the husband was complaisant. When he was not, other means were adopted.

At about 11:00 a.m. in the morning of the 10 June, 1907, the brother, Sripal Singh, together with the cousin and the village *chaukidar*, or watchman, arrived at the police station, which was eight miles away from the village, and reported the murder of Bhawar Singh. The following extracts from the report are the only passages of importance:

> *A low-caste menial who works at our place, called out this morning to Bhawar Singh, and got no reply. He climbed on to the roof to get the key, and found Bhawar Singh lying dead on the floor of the roof, with his throat cut, and several injuries on his body. Bhawar Singh used to live at the granary. I live at the dwelling-house. The menial came and called me. I went running to the place and found the throat*

cut, but partially joined with the skin. There were several injuries on the dead body, and the belly was cut through with the injuries. I raised an alarm, and several men of the village came up. When Lalli Mian saw this, he said he was going to the village of Khairaha to collect money there, and that he saw Atbal Singh, Munna Singh, Chheda Singh, Dhonda Singh, Prag Singh, Raghubir Singh, and Jag Mohan Singh, coming out hastily from the lane at the back of that house. Other men also who had come out to ease themselves at that time, also saw those men going. There was an old enmity between those men and my brother, and because of the same enmity they murdered him.

The seven men whose names are given in the report were all of them thakurs, the same caste as the deceased, and the same seven as those who were put on their trial. Further, the cause of the old enmity was discreetly left open. A discreet silence about the reason for the enmity, which is said to be the motive for the murder, means one of two things.

Either the persons making the report knew the real motive and withheld it, because it reflected upon the deceased and his family, or upon themselves, or they were not sure about it, or even about the real murderers, and they wished to leave a door open for retreat. The next feature of importance in the case was the medical evidence. The head was almost completely severed from the trunk. This was, of course, sufficient to cause death. The following additional injuries were described:

(a) The male organ was cut at its root, only one inch remaining.
(b) Both testicles were seen from the inside bone on either side of the scrotum.

(c) Nose was cut off in the middle, slicing off the upper-lip also.
(d) A big gaping wound over the right side of the chest, and cutting it and the sixth rib, tailing off on the right side of the abdomen.
(e) Three penetrating wounds on the abdomen close to the navel left side. From these four feet of the small intestine came out.
(f) Two cuts on the right shoulder.
(g) A cut on the right scapular region.
(h) The liver was cut on the inner side.

The report in this case contained two statements, which, though not as specific as one would wish, were of great importance.

It said, 'Death was due to mortal wounds on the neck, face, abdomen, chest, etc., haemorrhage and shock therefrom'. One can only conclude from this that the injuries to the body were inflicted during lifetime. The Civil Surgeon was not called at the trial, and this was the only piece of medical evidence. Yet the judge found that the body wounds must have been inflicted after death, and that the body must have been lifted off the cot, also after death, for the purpose. There was not a scrap of evidence to support this view, which was inconsistent with the only piece of medical evidence. Secondly, the report said, "The stomach contained about two ounces of semi-digested food – bread, mango, etc." It could hardly have been in a less-advanced stage of digestion than the articles specifically mentioned. The articles specifically mentioned are easily digested; certainly, in less than four hours. The a priori inference which most people would draw from this is, that the murder took place not more than four hours after the evening meal, and therefore before midnight. The importance of this point will become apparent. The evidence of Lalli Mian, cited in the report given above, put the hour of the murder at four o'clock in the morning.

The point of next importance was the geography. The ancestral house of the deceased was probably substantial, with a verandah, a courtyard, and a *zenana* or women's quarters. The place where he slept was a mere hut, with mud walls, and beams, and a flat roof plastered with mud, and jumbled up anyhow amidst other village mud huts. The lane at the back of it was not a real lane, but a mere narrow passage between two curtilages, or huts, wide enough perhaps for two persons to walk abreast with difficulty. Adjoining the house was one in ruins. Probably the roof had given way first, either through dry-rot in the beams, or through the weight of wind and water in the rains. As the roof gave way, it brought down the upper portions of the mud walls, and the little ruin stayed like that for years, because no one would take the trouble, or spend the money to rebuild it. The ruined wall adjoining the deceased's house, or granary, was less than three feet high.

•

When Salman was informed about the murder of Bhawar Singh, he immediately got into action. He spoke with the Sub-Inspector who told him that anyone could ascend to the roof of the granary with ease, and that there were marks to show that 'someone' climbed up to the roof from the wall of the ruin.

The expression 'someone' might have been important as indicating that there were marks of only one person; but the servant who discovered the corpse certainly climbed up somewhere, and the point was not pressed at the trial, though the Sub-Inspector clearly had one of the possible murderers in his mind when he referred to it. So many men had been up to the roof after the murder, before he arrived, that nothing could really be made of the footmarks. The only other point of importance in the geography was that the house of Badlu, with whose wife the deceased was alleged to have an intrigue, was only twenty paces away, and that the roof of the granary could easily be approached from it. The Sub-Inspector had some reason for examining with care the roof, and the parapet, and the walls of Badlu's house, but he found nothing.

The house of Badlu was two-storeyed, while the deceased's granary had only one storey, being about seven and a half feet high. There were seven or eight houses belonging to other village menials, close by, and the brother of the deceased said that in the month of June, most of these men slept on their roofs.

The brother of the deceased, Sripal Singh, was the first and principal witness for the prosecution, and gave evidence of the motive relied upon by the prosecution and accepted by the judge. He said, "There was once a fight between the deceased and the seven accused. This thing took place seven or eight years ago. There was a fight with *lathis* (the heavy, iron-bound bamboo stick) carried by many villager, a report was made, but the case was not taken to the court. My cousin-brother, Ajgar Singh got Atbal Singh, the principal accused and uncle of three of the others, fined on account of trespass. This happened five or six years ago."

He denied, in cross-examination, that he knew anything about an intrigue between the deceased and the wife of Badlu, or that he knew that some of Badlu's relatives had refused to dine with Badlu. The characteristic feature of his evidence about the enmity was the careful limitation of the fight, seven years before, to the deceased on the one side and the seven accused on the other. No one, however credulous, could possibly swallow this story as containing the whole truth. But this was all that the witness ever committed himself to.

The cousin-brother, Ajgar Singh, gave an entirely different account of the origin of the same enmity. He did not confirm about the seven-years-old fight, and his brother was not recalled to confirm the later version. The following is an extract from his evidence at the trial. It contains the perennial source of trouble arising from the same name for different villagers:

> "Atbal Singh (an accused) and Binda Singh, father of Prag Singh (an accused), are cousins. Jag Mohan Singh is of their party and is a relation also. Prag Singh and Raghubir Singh (an accused) are brothers. Atbal Singh is the uncle of Munna Singh, Dhonda Singh and Chheda Singh (accused). There was enmity between them and Bhawar Singh. On account of Bhawar Singh's influence, Atbal Singh, Chheda Singh, Dhondu Singh, Munna Singh, Raghubir Singh, Prag Singh, and Jag Mohan Singh did not get labourers. He used to stand up against these men whenever a case would crop up in the village. He was a zamindar and the mukhia of the village. There was a dispute between Dali and Raghubir over a woman. She had run away to Raghubir. She was related to Dali. Dali's mother had gone to ease herself. Raghubir beat her by mistake; Dali beat Raghubir then. The village assembled. Atbal Singh arrived and Bhawar Singh also arrived. Atbal Singh sided with Raghubir. Bhawar Singh sided with Dali. This led to a quarrel between Bhawar Singh and Atbal Singh. Atbal Singh said he will take out the bowels of Bhawar Singh, and Bhawar Singh said that he would take the eyes out of Atbal Singh.

In the meantime, my brother arrived, and took Bhawar Singh away. Reports were made on behalf of both and complaints filed. There was a compromise between Dali and Raghubir after Bhawar Singh's death. This quarrel between the two took place ten or twelve days before Bhawar Singh's death. Ten or fifteen labourers always worked at Bhawar Singh's land. He had eight plough boys. Others used to work in our family. So, these accused could not get any labourers. I am a member of the District Board. There is no other enmity besides the enmity I have stated. I never heard of Bhawar Singh's immoral character. I never heard about his keeping Badlu's wife, or about his connection with Badlu's daughter. He did not have any confidence in his servant. He therefore used to sleep in the house to look after the grain. His grain was never stolen. I learned from Badlu that he had slept on his own roof. I enquired about the time of the arrival of the Sub- Inspector. The deceased had told me that his life was in danger. Ten or twelve days before the murder, I had told him that Dali had told me that he was going from the village about eleven o'clock in the night, and that he had seen three men standing near the bed of the deceased, and that when he challenged them, they ran away. They were three of the accused, Munna Singh, Dhonda Singh, and Chheda Singh. I did not make any report at the police station. I had advised the deceased to have one or two men with him when he slept there.

He then, used to have men to sleep with him. I cannot say who. I did not see them. He told me so."

•

It is fairly certain that Ajgar Singh was wrong about men sleeping with the deceased, though the deceased may have made him believe it. If there had been any, they would almost certainly have been murdered. The fact that there were none, in the face of this evidence from the cousin-brother, is, to say the least of it, suggestive, but it appears to have been ignored in the very long judgment of the Sessions Judge.

The next witnesses, in importance, were the eyewitness who said they saw the accused about the time of the murder. The principal one was Lalli Mian, mentioned in the first information report. He was a Muslim, unconnected with either of the factions by caste or religion, and, as far as a villager in such a case is likely to be, independent. But he was a man of humble position, with a few acres of land for which he paid an annual rent of forty rupees. It was probably mortgaged, because he was in employment at a wage of only seven rupees per month. His statement was:

> "I was in Semari on the night of the murder. At about four o'clock in the morning I started for Khairaha. I had to pass by the front of the house where the deceased slept. I first went to ease myself. I then washed my hands. When I reached the house, I saw the seven accused coming out through the lane. They came from the enclosure at the back of the house. I then went to Khairaha, and returned an hour later. I heard crying in the house of the deceased, and learned that he had been murdered. I then gave the seven names."

In cross-examination he said, "There was no light when I left my house. The sun had not arisen then. There was no daylight, even when I washed my hands, or when I reached the house. The sun had risen when I reached Khairaha. I was once convicted for having eaten up a goat. Sheo Ratan complained against me. Atbal Singh (the accused) was a witness in the case against me. I was acquitted on appeal. I was convicted in a cattle theft case, and sentenced to one year's imprisonment. The accused passed five or six paces from me. They must have seen me. We did not speak, though we are on speaking terms. They held sticks and short clubs in their hands. I saw no stains on their clothing."

Dhuma Khan, another Mohammedan villager, was another witness examined. He said, "I had gone to Rithwan before dawn. I returned to the village about forty minutes after sunrise, and heard of the murder. On my way to Rithwan, I saw seven men going along the canal bank away from the village. Two were ahead, and I could not see who they were. I recognised the other five; the accused Atbal Singh, Munna Singh, Raghubir Singh, Prag Singh and Jag Mohan Singh.

I did not see Lalli Mian. They were going along quietly. I saw lathis and short clubs in their hands. I did not see any hatchet, gun, sword or axe with them. They walked faster when they saw me."

Ansuya Singh said, "On the morning of the murder, I saw Atbal Singh going away from the village with a gun on his shoulder. It was just about sunrise. He was about two hundred yards from the village. I am the brother of Ajgar Singh, and cousin-brother to Sripal Singh. There was no exchange of greetings between us. He was about eighty yards away. I saw him in the moonlight that had appeared."

Mehpal Singh, who was between sixty and seventy years old, said, "There is a pond near my house, which is about half a mile from the village, in another hamlet. On the morning of the murder, immediately after sunrise, I saw Atbal Singh washing his hands, his feet, and his shoes in that pond. He then went away with his gun. I am the uncle of Sripal Singh. My sight is not good, but I could recognise the form."

These last two witnesses, apart from being members of the murdered man's family and imbued with the enmity, were almost certainly what is known as 'police padding'. They were not cross-examined on the point. They may have been volunteers, being near relatives of the deceased and anxious to secure the conviction of the common enemy, and the gun was probably introduced to suggest that Atbal Singh, the principal accused, went out to lead the gang, carrying a gun to break down any resistance they might meet.

But the incident was typical of the lack of firm handling and clear thinking in the preparation of a criminal prosecution, because two witnesses had already been called who described in detail what the accused were carrying, and who must have seen the gun if there had been one. The explanation of Ansuya Singh that he could see Atbal Singh 'in the moonlight that had appeared' was an absurd excrescence, because the incident occurred, according to him, at sunrise, when it would be daylight.

Salman searched the houses of the accused and took a statement from Badlu's wife, but she was not called. He explained his procedure in the following way,

"Someone had said that there was an intimacy between the deceased and Badlu's wife, so I examined her. I learned that the deceased's nose and male organ had been entirely removed. I don't remember how this fact was taken by me at the time. I did not form any opinion at the time that some woman was at the bottom of the case. I examined others besides Badlu's wife and asked the accused if they would give any evidence of it."

Badlu, who was a vegetable grower said, "On the night on which Bhawar Singh died, I was sleeping on my roof. My roof is twenty or twenty-two paces from Bhawar Singh's roof. On that night I rose to answer nature's call. It was early morning. Then I heard the sound of thuds. I looked in all directions. Then I saw seven persons on the roof of Bhawar Singh's house. I recognised them. I called Bhawar and asked him who were on his roof. On this Munna Singh, Raghubir Singh, and Chheda Singh came to my roof. Munna Singh had a *kulhari* (axe). Chheda Singh had a lathi. They said they would kill me if I did not keep quiet. Then Prag Singh, Dhondu Singh, and Atbal Singh jumped out from the enclosure. I did not recognise the seventh man. The three persons who came to me fled away when the other four leaped out. It was an hour before sunrise. I then came down from my roof in fright. I remained in my house on the next day. I did not go out because of fear. I met Ajgar Singh and Sripal Singh in the evening.

I am married. There was no intimacy between my wife and Bhawar Singh. I do not know what time Bhawar Singh came to bed. The men had surrounded his charpoy. I could not see if he was on it or on the ground. I did not go to my roof in the morning. About half an hour after sunrise I heard of the murder. But I did not come out of my house for fear. I heard that there were many villagers assembled round the corpse. Sripal Singh and Ajgar Singh told me to tell the truth as they knew I had been on the roof."

The only observation to be made about this part of his evidence was that it was difficult to see why he should have felt any fear, unless he had an idea that he would be suspected of having been concerned in the murder, though hiding in his house would hardly serve to remove this suspicion. The remainder of the case for the prosecution consisted of the two witnesses who were parties to the strange incident about Raghubir's wife, which was said by the witness Ajgar Singh, the cousin brother of the deceased, to have constituted the main source of enmity between the deceased and the accused.

Dali was cultivator and tender of cattle in the village, and was eighteen years of age. He said, "I had a threshing-floor this year. Bhawar Singh also had his *khalihan* (threshing floor) half a door from my floor. During the time of threshing, we used to sleep in our respective khalihans. Twenty-five or twenty-six days before Bhawar Singh's death, Chheda Singh, Munna Singh, and Dhonda Singh were going towards Bhawar Singh's bed at midnight. Bhawar Singh was sleeping in his bed. I had gone to the khalihan from my house. I challenged who were near Bhawar Singh's. I got no reply; the men fled towards the south. The three men had lathis in their hands. Next morning, I told Bhawar Singh what I had seen.

I had once had a quarrel with Raghubir. His wife's sister used to live with him. She fled away and came to me. Then she fled away from my house. Raghubir came to me and asked me if his wife's sister was in my house. I replied she was not at my house. She did come, but she ran away. He insisted on my giving her to him. I said how could I. Atbal Singh on behalf of Raghubir told me, "Why don't you give her to Raghubir?" He abused me. I said she is not here. Then Atbal Singh abused me and threatened to beat me. Bhawar Singh told Atbal Singh, "Why are you threatening him?" Atbal Singh said to Bhawar Singh, "If you will interrupt, I will tear you apart." This talk took place six or seven days before the murder. I made a report of this affair. The police came to enquire. Raghubir then brought a complaint against me in the Deputy Sahib's court. I too made a complaint. Bhawar Singh sided with me, and Raghubir was supported by Atbal Singh. The cases were finished after Bhawar Singh's death. These cases were compromised.

•

It will be noticed that he put the incident – when he saw three of the accused apparently threatening the deceased – more than three weeks before the murder. Ajgar Singh had stated that it was ten or twelve days before the murder.

Raghubir himself, when he was called to testify, did the case more harm than good for the prosecution. He flatly denied that any dispute took place between the deceased and the accused, Atbal, on the subject. He said,

"I had a quarrel with Dali over my wife. She was my former wife's sister. I then married her. I complained against Dali. I made a report at the police station. He made a report against me. When I caught hold of my wife, Dali rescued her and took her. He brought my wife to my house. My wife lived in Dali's possession. He might have kept her anywhere. All the village was there. There was no quarrel in the village. There was no quarrel between Atbal Singh and Bhawar Singh when I caught hold of my wife. They did not threaten one another."

The first witness for the defence was Wahid Ali, a sheikh and a zamindar of the village, who gave his age as sixty-five. He said,

"Bhawar Singh was a gambler and a whoremonger. It was rumoured that he carried on with Badlu's wife for a long time. Once a former chaukidar reported at the police station that Bhawar Singh and Badlu's wife were found together. A summons was sent from the police station. The woman was in hiding for a month. Badlu has two daughters. I know nothing about them. Members of his caste have refused to eat with him. A meeting was held, and they stopped social communication on account of the intrigue.

I was head constable in the police force. I retired ten years ago. Badlu's wife is about forty. My informants were my tenants. I advised Bhawar Singh many times to give up his evil habits. Three years ago, I sued Barkat Ali and Bhawar Singh appeared as a witness for him. I never saw any intimacy between Bhawar Singh and Badlu's wife."

The fact, admitted by the witness, that the deceased had appeared as a witness against him in some case three years ago would be considered quite sufficient to shake his credit in saying anything against the dead man's character.

Durga Dayal, a member of the same caste as the deceased and the accused, went further. He said, "Bhawar Singh was a bad character. He had intimacy with Badlu's wife. He kept Badlu's eldest daughter married in Fatehpur. He would not let her go with her husband for a year. Her husband took her away by force. Budhu, Badlu's son, once told Sripal that the deceased had raped his youngest sister. Badlu has been excommunicated. When he returned from Gaya (after some religious rites) he gave a dinner, but no member of his caste would eat with him."

"I used to see the deceased always at Badlu's house in the last seven or eight years. He used to be familiar with her in the presence of Budhu, and also Badlu. Bhawar Singh would not leave a woman alone, be she old or lame or blind. Badlu tolerated his wife's misconduct. Budhu, her son, did not."

•

The next three witnesses were important because they were members of the same caste of vegetable growers and sellers as Badlu. Jagua said,

"Badlu's wife is a bad lot. She was intimate with the deceased. I don't smoke or eat with Badlu. He has been excommunicated. Badlu's son-in-law once came for the eldest daughter, who was his wife, but the deceased would not let her go. He complained to everyone, but we could be of no help. The eldest daughter was allowed to go last year. I heard some months ago that Budhu complained to Sripal Singh that the deceased had taken his mother's honour, and now wished to dishonour his sister, and that no one took any notice of it."

"Badlu's excommunication took place some years ago. I did not personally see Bhawar Singh having a connection with Badlu's wife. I did go to a meeting of the caste, because Badlu had raped my daughter. I paid him back in his own coin. I also raped Badlu's eldest daughter. This was two years ago. I have not been excommunicated for this. I am a tenant of Prag Singh, accused. I also pay rent to Sripal Singh, brother of the deceased."

Three witnesses for the defence gave evidence to similar effect and alleged that Badlu had been excommunicated on account of his wife's conduct. One of them was the mukhia of the caste and, one would think, ought to be trusted to tell the truth. Another of the three said that Badlu's wife had so much influence with Badlu that he could do nothing with her, and that when she was challenged at the meeting of the caste, she became angry and abused them all, so that they, in their turn, 'became angry and went away'.

All seven accused were examined in much the same way.

Q: *Lalli Mian says that he saw you in a lane in front of Bhawar Singh's cattle house on Sunday night. What do you say?*
A: *His statement is false.*

Q: *Badlu says that he saw you on Bhawar Singh's roof on Sunday night. What do you say?*
A: *His statement is false.*

Q. *Dhuman Khan says that he saw you at Rotie ghat. What do you say?*

A. *His statement is false.*

Q. *Dali says that you at one time sided with Raghubir, when he and Dali had a quarrel over Raghubir's wife. Also, that you threatened Bhawar Singh.*
A. *His statement is false.*

Q. *Ansuya Singh says that he saw you going with a gun to Kalrawapur on Sunday morning?*
A. *His statement is untrue.*

Q. *Mehpal Singh says that he saw you washing your hands, feet and shoes on Sunday morning in a pond near his house.*
A. *His statement is false.*

Q. *Why do Lalli, Badlu, Dhuman Khan, Dali, Ansuya and Mehpal speak against you?*
A. *Lalli had eaten up Sheo Ratan's goat. I appeared as a witness against him. Badlu's wife was intimate with Bhawar Singh. I appeared as a witness against Badlu in a panchayat. Dhuman had cut a mohwa tree from my grove. My son beat him. Dali is under Sripal's influence. Ansuya is the brother of Sripal, Mehpal is his uncle.*

Q. *Where were you between Saturday and Sunday?*
A. *I was at Calcutta. I returned home on Tuesday, ten days after the murder.*

Q. *Was Bhawar Singh killed?*
A. *Yes.*

Q. *Who killed him?*

A. *Bhawar Singh was close to Badlu's wife and daughter. Badlu might have killed him or Budhu.*

The judge was not convinced about the intrigue, but the reasons he gave for deciding this issue definitely in the negative were not convincing. As a matter of fact, his ultimate decision was equivalent to treating it as irrelevant, which is probably the correct view. But the issue of the deceased's intrigue, relied upon by the defence, undoubtedly had great influence with the assessors, all of whom said that they thought the case was not proved against any of the accused. They must have thought that if they believed the defence story of the intrigue, it was an answer to the charge. The judge himself took this view in his judgment.

The enmity of the accused towards the deceased may have been the primary cause of their desire to get rid of him, and his evil reputation may well have been the decisive one. The judge found that the alleged quarrel and threats between the deceased and Atbal Singh, the accused, over Raghubir's wife were true, and further, that there had been enmity for some years. He also found that the evidence of the four witnesses Lalli Mian, Badlu, Ansuya Singh, and Mehpal Singh was true. In that case, the evidence of motive became quite unimportant.

The evidence of Badlu, if accepted, was in itself decisive, apart from the fact that it was corroborated. But when the judge came to the question of the guilt or innocence of each separate accused, he fell back upon the motive, and he acquitted Prag Singh, Jag Mohan Singh and Raghubir Singh. But all of them were mentioned by the witness Lalli, against whom little was shown to his discredit. Plus, all of them, except Jag Mohan Singh, were seen by Badlu, who saw seven on the roof, though he failed to recognise the seventh.

Salman was not convinced with the outcome. Although all three of those acquitted were included in the story of the ancient enmity which the judge accepted, he held that neither of them had any motive for committing the murder. It is difficult to follow the logic of this conclusion, or to regard it as having been other than a sort of compromise.

5

The Murder of the Watchdog

Offences pertaining to matrimonial fidelity have been one of the most common causes of murder in all ages.

In the nineteenth century, when child marriage and polygamy were common among the rich, the disparity in age between husband and wife was a potent factor. A man of thirty-five would be betrothed to a child of nine. They saw very little of each other till the latter attained puberty. By then, the man would be over forty, and had become blasé.

As a rule, the man would not take his bride to a home of their own, but to his parents' abode, where the girl has to turn to relieve her mother-in-law of all the household drudgery, and subject herself to the old couple without a murmur. The husband goes out to his work and returns in the evening. Then, he bathes at the well, and sings out for his dinner which is the wife's especial business to prepare. Woe betides her if the meal is not ready, or not to her lord's liking. She is not permitted to eat while he eats, and usually squats in the background, in anxiety, fearing lest he should find fault with her culinary efforts.

The first shortcoming in this respect may be tackled with words, in which the parents-in-law join, but a repetition of the offence is punished by an application of the stick, a measure applauded and approved of by the old people. So, it goes on; the girl becomes hardened by constant ill-usage, and there being no sentiment on either side, the chances of reconciliation are remote. She now contrives to acquire more time to herself; she goes out, mingles with the other girls of the village, and smarting under the sense of her unhappy lot at home, she looks around for someone to console her. Eventually, she meets a young fellow more of her own age. She is seen talking to him; the mother-in-law hears of it, divines the truth, and knowing that taxing the girl with her conduct would be of no avail, she informs her son. Enraged though he is, he will take no immediate action till he catches his wife. He dissembles; he lies in wait, watches and – succeeds.

He allows him to escape while the stab of a knife, the blow of a club – usually the household rice-pounder – or a constriction of the throat settles his erring wife for all time. The neighbours, on learning of the provocation, say she deserved her fate, and the homicide has their sympathy.

The police take up the matter and the murderer is hunted down and arrested. He is hauled before the sessions judge; the judge announces sentence, delivers him to the officer, and the officer hangs him. If it is the other way about, and the woman is the aggrieved party, she does one of two things – she either raises a scene by tearing her hair and proclaiming her wrongs to the whole village, or she reserves it for her spouse. Pretending to think nothing about it, she decks herself out in her best clothes. She puts flowers in her hair, anoints her person with precious spikenard, cooks a particularly tasty meal and lays herself out to be pleasant on the husband's return home. When her husband has dined, she mysteriously produces some arrack, which she tells him she has smuggled in unknown to the old parents.

The husband quaffs the fiery splint and falls into a heavy sleep, whereupon she takes some sharp, pointed instrument, previously prepared and straightway prods him to the heart. The man dies with scarcely a struggle. Then, she steals out, and either goes to her parental home, or takes refuge with some friend. Whichever it is, the murder is soon discovered. She is speedily run to earth and the village authorities are notified. Then, the police come in, take the girl to the lock-up, and in due course, she is sentenced to the gallows.

•

This is one such story. Rukmini Devi was the well-to-do zamindar of Kumhrar village. She had become a widow at the age of eleven, having been married to the aged zamindar Ramakant Choudhary when she was hardly nine. After the death of her husband twenty-two years ago, she had become the zamindar of Kumhrar village. The other wives of her late husband had all died without leaving any son to claim any share in the zamindari.

The only brother of her dead husband had been sent to gallows seven years ago, charged with the murder of his own wife, whom he had caught red-handed with one of their cooks. Rukmini Devi had inherited almost a dozen villages. She was young and had great personal attraction. She had kept teachers to learn both Hindi and English languages and was able to converse on her own with the local Sub-Divisional Magistrate (SDM) in Queen's language. She had even attended a few parties at the English club in Patna and had acquired a veneer of western manners. An aristocratic Indian lady, she had groomed herself in this way but she lacked the artificiality and rather pronounced self-assertiveness and over confidence of her more westernised sister. She retained the artlessness of a child of nature. She moved amongst her circle of friends like a timid fawn, with a strange mixture of shyness and responsiveness, almost plaintive playfulness.

Beneath the external polish and grace lurked an uncouth and surprisingly repellent exhibition of mannerisms, observable in one who whitened her teeth and reddened her tongue and gums to the hue of freshly-shed blood by chewing betel-nut, and who had learned neither the use of a handkerchief nor an aversion to expectoration. Under her gentle, winning smile and fair skin smouldered the latent fires of an inherited savagery. She was capable of cold-blooded cruelty and ruthless brutality, especially to the one who had offended her. And, of malice and if her jealousy should be awakened. Her mind suffered keenly from the pangs of jealousy, which was rather quickly aroused. She often steeped in religious and political bigotry and in a narrow-minded vindictiveness towards her neighbour or an erring servant.

•

Sometimes, Rukmini Devi seemed to be little more than a child, but she had great force of character. She was naturally vivacious and full of humour, and could be entertaining and charming when she pleased. She also had an iron will and determination above the average of her class. She broke the purdah whenever it suited her to do so, although she preserved the appearance of it, partly from habit, and partly from a feminine appreciation of its value as a weapon, both in defence and attack.

Being a young childless widow, she had acquired an unusual degree of independence. She lived for the most part, particularly during the hot weather, in a large two-storied house in Kumhrar.

This house was of modern construction, with many western amenities and was part of her inheritance. She had secured possession of her property after a long and desperate struggle. She had been engaged for years in prolonged and complicated litigation forced upon her by rival claimants. They used several methods for asserting their claims, aided by the tortuous and bewildering processes.

The rival claimants were some distant relatives of her deceased husband, whose claim to property was some ancestral mistake of naming the successor. The legal process had quickened her intelligence and fostered a natural inclination to free herself from the fetters of seclusion which bind the majority of her class. She had emerged from it triumphant, but her victory had left her surrounded by enemies whose defeats had not diminished their venom or their desire for vengeance even though they had exhausted their resources. This was a familiar phenomenon of most landed families and of litigation over estates. The defeated litigant, however slender or imaginary his claims, always remained the aggrieved party, and nursed schemes for retaliation. Even Rukmini Devi expected to meet her enemies again in some new field which chance or their own ingenuity might provide for a renewal of their attacks upon her peaceful existence.

She kept up a substantial domestic establishment, in addition to the extensive cultivation machinery for her land. One of her servants, Bhagwati, had been a faithful servant to her household. He had disappeared for the last few days, and all efforts by Rukmini Devi as well as the local police to trace him had been futile. Bhagwati's role in the domestic household was that of a watchdog. He would accompany Rukmini Devi whenever she ventured out for business. While at home, he would sleep between the main entrance door and the main staircase leading to the upper floor, and to keep watch lest any persons who had no business there should attempt to enter the house at night. These instructions were unusual and peculiar.

They were given to Bhagwati alone, though if he was like the ordinary servant, he made no secret about them with his associates. But Bhagwati was given no companion in his night watch. Rukmini Devi had no special reason to fear an attack by dacoits. If she had, her precautions were quite inadequate for protecting her house and its inmates, or her property. Dacoits invariably came at night in large bands, with firearms and other lethal weapons; with torches, straw and paraffin, and proceeded to their work, after frightening away all the villagers and inmates of the house by a sort of preliminary bombardment in the air with their rifles. A well-armed body of villagers or servants was required to stop them. Once they entered, they set fire to anyone they caught, beat and tortured them until they disclosed where the portable property was concealed. After stripping the zenana of the jewellery, they worked their will upon the bodies of the defenceless women. It was almost inconceivable that the idea of a raid by a band of robbers entered into the mind of either Bhagwati or his mistress.

Bhagwati was an old and trusted servant and he faithfully carried out his mistress' orders. It was always believed that it was to this fidelity that he owed his death. Anyhow, he had suddenly disappeared. One point about his disappearance was clear. Although his absence must have been generally remarked throughout the household, little or no notice was taken of it at the time. He was, on the whole, an indoor servant with certain definite outdoor duties. On the day of his disappearance, he must have been missed several times before nightfall. There were many servants and other people in the house as well, who for different reasons, were equally interested in keeping silent – some because they knew too much about the cause of his disappearance, and others because they knew too little, and hoped they could learn more by waiting. Perhaps, the strangest fact of all in the series of strange events which subsequently came to light was that even Rukmini Devi herself said nothing. If she learned anything from any inquiries which she made, she kept quiet about it, and took no steps to ascertain what had happened to her faithful servant. If amongst subordinates, there are some who have been up to some mischief, and the situation is such where information is sought, everyone wishes to know the other's extent of ignorance or knowledge on the matter at hand.

On the fourth day of Bhagwati's disappearance, Rukmini Devi went to the village where her own parents and brothers lived. She had left late in the afternoon in a bullock-cart, taking with her a maid-servant and a quantity of her jewellery and other personal belongings, evidently with the intention of making a long stay. The month was October. The weather was beginning to cool; and the big house in which she had been living, and in which these events had happened, did not suit her during the cold weather. She had written to her elder brother informing him of her plans, but the letter had not reached him.

•

No report was made to the police station about the mysterious disappearance of Bhagwati. But, this course is seldom taken without the cooperation either of the mukhia or of the leading zamindar if he is in residence. No one was likely to intervene at this stage about an incident in the zamindar's house, in which nothing had occurred to give publicity to the matter, unless the zamindar did so himself. As a result, there was no 'First Report', which is generally an important feature in criminal cases in India, and no immediate investigation.

The absence of FIR made it a very tricky case for the police to follow through. The statements the First Information Report (FIR) contains are not allowed to be treated as evidence of the facts alleged in it. However, it is universally admitted, and largely used, as a means of checking the statements made in evidence by the witnesses for the prosecution. Over generations, a traditional practice has grown up making free use of it. The line between its illegitimate use as actual evidence and its legitimate use as a mere document of reference has been worn so thin as to be almost impalpable. The reason for this is obvious.

The story the FIR contains is very often cooked. Sometimes, it is a mere hash of half-truths and hearsay which the chaukidar has made up in his head on his journey to the thana. But more often, it is a carefully prepared summary of the view of the crime which the village, led by the mukhia or by the leading zamindar, desires to be taken by the police.

•

The police's first task was to discover whether it bears any relation to the real facts at all. If the case is a straightforward one, and the criminal is known to the villagers and they wish him to be caught and punished, the first report is generally straightforward too. But, the villagers themselves are so often anxious to shield the culprit and to confuse the police or to start a positively false case, that apprehensive consultations take place before a decision is taken as to what shall be reported, and the chaukidar is sent off with a meticulously constructed cock-and-bull tale.

This may happen with the complicity of the mukhia, who as headman, is morally responsible for making some effort to discover the criminal, and who can always protect himself from the charge of having made a false case by pleading that it was hearsay and all that he could learn at the time.

Or it may happen through the agency of some leading members of a party interested in concealing the truth, who succeed in getting hold of the chaukidar, and in sending him off with the prepared story before anyone else can tamper with him. It follows therefore, that the distance from the village to the thana and the interval of time occupied in sending off the chaukidar on foot, are points of real importance which every criminal court is bound to examine with care. The distance is generally several miles at least, and chaukidars, especially at night and in the small hours of the morning, do not hurry themselves.

The absence of an FIR nearly always means that those who would naturally be the first to make a complaint are themselves involved in the commission of the crime, or are anxious to cover it up. Every class of crime ought to be reported.

•

Time passed. Rukmini Devi did not return from her father's house and the existence and disappearance of Bhagwati seemed to have been forgotten. Some of his friends believed that he had gone to Burma with one of the numerous labour parties, where money and adventure were to be found. This case seemed to have come to a dead end which was very frustrating for police.

Sundar, another servant of Rukmini Devi, had been gossiping overtime to give fuel to this impression. Sundar claimed when confronted by Bhagwati's relatives that he had never said so because he did not know. He had merely conjectured it in the most casual way as the possible explanation of the mysterious disappearance. But, it was very unlikely that Bhagwati would have departed in this way all of a sudden, even for the adventurous exploit of joining the labour parties to Burma where a number of labourers from adjoining villages had been going for clearing forests in Burma as lot of teak was required for the ever-growing railway network in India at that time. But, it was highly unlike Bhagwati to leave without saying a word to his family or to his fellow servants. More so without making any disposition of his property or communicating with his brother, Behari Lai. His pair of shoes, although of trifling value, he would have been almost certain to take with him, because Indian servants are very careful of their possessions.

•

Behari Lal was not content with the assurances he had received about Bhagwati's safety. One day, he confronted Sundar about this Burma trip but Sundar readily changed his statement. To Behari, Sundar repeatedly asserted that Bhagwati had gone off with a woman with whom he had been carrying on, although he already had two wives. It was on this account, he said, that no hue and cry had been raised, or serious search was made. The suggestion of him having gone to Burma, though consistent with his restless and adventurous disposition, was only put forward to prevent the necessity of telling the truth, and thereby bringing shame on his name and family.

Behari Lai was much disturbed by this story, but gave it little credence. He could not understand what sort of liaison his brother could have formed without his knowledge. Also, why he should have suddenly gone off in this way, without his clothes and the only pair of shoes. He returned to Rukmini Devi's house again and again with sullen obstinacy, repeating his inquiries and getting the same vague explanations from the other servants. He eventually traced the shoes to one of the servants, Jhoku, a low-caste fellow, from whose house he recovered them. All that Jhoku would say was that he had received them from Sundar after Bhagwati had left. This was strenuously denied by Sundar.

Behari Lai also saw what he believed to be his brother's lathi. He espied it in the hand of Jhoku's mother. This was awkward for Jhoku, but here, consideration of caste came into play. Behari would not claim the lathi, saying that Jhoku must have used it for their pigs. The idea of his lathi having been used for stirring up pigs would be abhorrent to a man of high caste, and if he handled it, or used it again, and the fact became known, he might have trouble with his caste-fellows. Behari Lai had come upon some promising clues. If he really wished to learn about his brother's fate and, the event of foul play being established to bring the culprits to justice, he had every inducement to report his suspicions to the police. However, he continued in the state of stolid indifference and dilatoriness, and allowed the matter to sleep. This inaction contributed to the difficulties which were experienced in the subsequent investigation.

The cold weather passed and it was getting well on into the following year. During this time, rumours of one kind and another were started. Once any suspicion reached them, the local enemies of Rukmini Devi saw the chance they had been waiting for. Eventually, they set the police in motion.

•

Salman came down to the village to make independent inquiries. He clearly had a difficult task. Not only had the lapse of time blurred any clues which might help him, but it had allowed so many strange stories to obtain a footing that it was difficult to decide which of them was worth following up.

The behaviour of Behari Lai made it doubtful whether any reliance could be placed on his story about the shoes and the lathi. And, the enmity against Rukmini Devi was so pronounced in the quarter from which his information had originally come as to make an experienced officer sceptical about the statements made to him. Very slight pressure by the neighbours and a few rupees from an interested partisan will induce a villager to make almost any wild statement to an investigation officer.

The common rumour in the village was that Rukmini Devi had procured the murder of her own servant with the assistance of Jhoku, who worked in the fields, and who was alleged to have taken part in the removal and burial of the corpse. It was even reported that Jhoku had admitted as much. This was highly unlikely, but common rumour in a village, especially in the case of a mystery of old standing, although mixed with palpably unreliable information, is very often not far from the truth.

Every experienced officer fully understands this, and his usual method of starting to work is to settle down in the village for a few days as its guest, and to gather around him knots of men whom he induces to talk with a certain amount of freedom by applying means best known to himself.

The villagers soon find that sullen silence does not pay. Police officials like to be handsomely treated, as well as to be held in awe, and a prolonged visit is apt to become embarrassing and expensive. 'Permission to be present' is given to all who are likely to be able to add to the general fund of information. The official would gather all such people under a shady tree and get as much information as possible. Thus, those who do not avail themselves of the 'permission' are likely to find themselves the object of attentions by the officer.

•

From the mass of contradictory gossips and rumours which the officer patiently gathers in the course of these little conferences, he is generally able to extract the least common denominator which puts him on to a solid line of inquiry. If there were any truth at all in the common village rumour in this case, it was certain that only one motive could have led the lady, or her satellites, to perpetrate such a cold-blooded murder. The dead man had no possessions and no enemies, and there was no obvious reason why anyone should desire his death, except to close his mouth.

By degrees, Salman learned that there were villagers who were prepared to prove that Rukmini Devi was in the habit of receiving a particular visitor at night. It was said that a young and wealthy zamindar named Bishan Singh, who lived in the neighbouring village, and who used to call openly by day for the purpose of making collections for some charitable object, would ride over after dark. He would leave his horse at a distance in charge of one of the lady's servants, and stay the night, leaving again on horseback in the early hours of the morning.

It was also said that letters were carried from Rukmini Devi to Bishan Singh and Sundar was the go-between. The visits of Bishan Singh had become more frequent just about the time of Bhagwati's disappearance when he continued to arrive as usual at night, and carried a revolver, along with a short sword or dagger.

•

Salman was not confident about this story, and the only persons who could provide direct evidence of it were the servants of the lady herself. Some of them had been heard to complain that they were not getting enough to eat so Salman turned his attention to that. He heard that the body of the missing man had been disposed of within the boundaries of the village, on the property of Rukmini

Devi, and a certain disused shed on the cultivator holding would repay a search. Accompanied by one of the members of the rival party, who may be described as 'the other side', the officer went to the shed. There, he found a bad smell in which there was a distinct suggestion of decomposed flesh and also a portion of earth which was exceptionally soft and yielding to pressure.

This was somewhat odd because if Bhagwati had been murdered and buried there, it had been done so long ago that this sort of indication was not to be expected. The place was opened up but nothing was discovered. Nor did it appear that the smell was any stronger when the earth was opened than it had been when the surface was undisturbed. This, however, did not deter Salman. He was now satisfied that he was on the eve of important discoveries which might make his reputation in the force. He sent a specimen of the soft earth to the official chemical examiner.

The analysis was favourable and it seemed probable that someone, who had been watching Salman's labours, had removed the remains and substituted fresh earth. Efforts were made to discover the spot to which such remains had been removed, but they produced nothing. It seemed clear, however that Jhoku, in whose possession the shoes were alleged to have been found, was the next scent to be followed. Only him, and other men of similar low caste, could be induced to handle a corpse. As a result, Salman turned his detective energies towards Jhoku. His efforts were not long in bearing fruit.

Finally, and probably not until after various threats and other forms of persuasion had been used upon him, Jhoku confessed, and disclosed an almost incredible murder in broad daylight. It must have been known to all the servants, in which he himself had filled the modest role of a sympathetic spectator and corpse concealer. This, by the way, is the invariable line taken by a subordinate who is the first to confess. He represents himself as an involuntary participator, generally compelled by threats to play the subordinate part assigned to him and threatened with his life if he tells the truth.

•

It is often a nice question whether his statement amounts to a confession which he can be brought to repeat before a magistrate, but the police take no risks. Whether the man is going to be charged or to be put up as a witness, he is invariably sent to a magistrate so that his 'confession' may be recorded.

Jhoku began his sensational story with a circumstantial account of the intrigue between Rukmini Devi and Bishan Singh. It was clear, he could only have been repeating what he had been told and what had long been current gossip in the village. Jhoku, in order to disarm criticism on this head, added corroborative details of his own. He was able to say that when Bishan Singh came on one of his nightly visits, he was admitted by the indoor servants and went upstairs. He said he used to follow him to the living rooms on the upper floor occasionally. He gave no reason for having done so, but his motive for saying it was probably not unconnected with the further statement that Bishan Singh used to put his sword and revolver away in a niche in the wall. In this way, he said that he would be able to recognise them if he saw them again.

The importance of this will be evident. But the improbability of anything of the kind, having been seen by Jhoku himself, was considerable. He was only an outdoor servant, who did odd jobs and helped look after the cows. There was no conceivable reason why the other servants should allow him to enter the house at night during clandestine visits to his mistress by her lover, and this part of the story was certainly a pure invention. It was deliberately put into his statement by an official who recorded his statement.

•

The first thing a police officer, with a 'find' like Jhoku in his hands, thinks of is to secure what he considers corroboration of the statement or confession, in case he wants to use him as an approver. This way, he is often guilty of the mistake of being overkeen, and of inserting statements, by way of supposed corroboration. The night preceding the day when Bhagwati was last seen alive, continued Jhoku, Bishan Singh had ridden over. He had found difficulty in obtaining an entrance into the house. He had called to Raja Ram, one of the older indoor servants, who had come to the door to open it and who had been forbidden to do so by Bhagwati.

Eventually, the young zamindar had been admitted and had stayed the night. He had left in the morning without his short sword. Nothing had occurred the next day until noon, when Raja Ram came running to Bhagwati crying that a big snake had been discovered in the house. Jhoku was sitting with Bhagwati when Raja Ram asked him to come and try to kill the snake. Bhagwati went off with Raja Ram, who told the other two to go back to their work. A little while afterwards, while he was with Baldeo looking after the bullocks, Jhoku had been called to the house.

He was taken upstairs to one of the uninhabited rooms which led to an inner room or closet. There, he saw the dead body of Bhagwati, cut up in pieces, which were lying on the floor of the inner room. Sundar and Raja Ram were there with another man whom he did not know and they appeared to be engaged in separating the limbs of the dead servant. Raja Ram had Bishan Singh's sword in his hand. The place was in a ghastly mess, the floor being covered with fresh blood which was still oozing from Bhagwati's body.

•

In the outer room stood Rukmini Devi, directing operations, and showing no more concern than if it were an ordinary occurrence upon which the men were engaged. There was a sack there with some string, and Jhoku and the unknown man were ordered to tie the pieces of the bleeding trunk in the sacking, and take it away and place it in a corner of another room. When it grew dark, they were asked to take it out and bury it in the ground in the disused shed. Having removed the corpse as they were told, they were then ordered to get some water and wash the floor. Rukmini Devi herself saw these orders carried out.

After all signs of the crime had been removed except the sack, Rukmini Devi had left in the bullock cart to join her father's family, while Raja Ram had supervised the disposal of the remains in the evening. The body had been buried at the spot where Salman had the earth dug, but shortly before his arrival, Jhoku had been ordered to assist in removing the decomposed remains to another place, where he understood they had been burned and re-buried. Some traces of burned bones and a small piece of sacking were unearthed by the officer from a hole in the ground near the spot which Jhoku pointed out to him and Jhoku professed to identify the sacking.

•

This was the story of the murder as related by the only available witness and upon which Salman now had to work. Apart from the other features of the case, the position of Jhoku was such that, having regard to his admitted complicity and his long silence, it was impossible that any court would accept his evidence against persons of apparent respectability unless it was amply corroborated. The character and position of the principal accused made the story almost incredible on the face of it. It would be difficult to persuade anyone that a young and gentle lady of good birth and education could have taken part in such a horrible crime. Still less did it seem credible that she would have had the nerve to witness the act of butchery. If there were any truth in the suggestion of a clandestine intrigue, it seemed the height of folly and a useless precaution to destroy the man whom she herself had set to watch. If anyone was likely to do that, it would surely be her paramour. But, there were other ways less ruthless and risky in which Bhagwati could have been tackled. There was nothing to indicate why he should have been left alone all day and then, murdered in cold blood. And it was strange that Bishan Singh's sword was used. Although its identification by Jhoku, if this could be arranged, might be treated by a court as some corroboration of this part of his evidence, it involved the conclusion that Bishan Singh had deliberately left it behind for the purpose and that he was in the confidence of the principal culprit. But men do not present their mistresses with weapons to commit murder for them, which they are not prepared themselves to commit. The sword was a dramatic touch which lent colour to the story of the intrigue and provided convincing proof of the motive. Honestly, on reflection, it had the appearance of being over done.

Nor did it seem probable that a cold-blooded murderess would leave the scene of the crime with the body still undisposed of. There was a clear risk of a mistake on the part of stupid servants which would hopelessly involve her. Moreover, the very enmity which had fostered the suspicion against the lady and had led to the discovery of such evidence as the police now had, would rightly be held to throw doubt and suspicion upon the source from which that evidence came. The method adopted for carrying out the murder was clumsy and unconvincing.

A total and unexpected disappearance, without any attempt to account for it, followed by indifference and silence, would be thought by intelligent criminals to be certain to provoke inquiries and to create an awkward atmosphere of mystery. Baldly put, the whole story seemed too good to be true. The belated testimony of a low-born menial – who could be notoriously easy to persuade to give false evidence and whose alleged knowledge of the circumstances could only have been acquired from criminal complicity – would never be accepted as sufficient to condemn a woman for such an act. This, or something like it, must have been the train of reasoning in Salman's mind as he reviewed the situation.

In the course of a search through the house of Rukmini Devi, he came upon what looked like a valuable piece of evidence. He found some passionate love letters and verses in a box which was said to belong to Rukmini Devi, written in Hindi, in the handwriting of an educated man. One of these were put in evidence at the trial. The others were love couplets, undated and unsigned.

Pearl of Beauty,

My love to you. We have not lived in vain. May the gods protect you and be propitious for my next journey. If this should not reach your hands and the faithful one is not seen here, I shall know. He must not speak with anyone here. I will see to it. Otherwise, he will return. The condition of my horse is the cause of much anxiety to me. He will require

> *attention. I hope much that it will not be long. You should make all ready. The thought of you is always with me and your absence is much felt. In my dreams your eyes shine like stars. But what is this to our waking hours, when the sky is clear and the clouds have passed away for a season? May god keep you in good health.*

Before taking any further step, the Sub-Inspector in-charge of the inquiry satisfied himself that he could obtain evidence to prove that these love letters were in the handwriting of Bishan Singh. He then sought an interview with Rukmini Devi. He gave her enough hints to understand, without disclosing what the evidence was, that there was grave reason to believe that she was concerned in the undoubted death by violence of the missing Bhagwati. If the Sub-Inspector had been liable to be influenced by monetary considerations, the case was one out of which he might have expected to do rather well. Rukmini Devi, like most wealthy zamindars in similar circumstances, would be easily persuaded to pay a large sum to get the case dropped for want of sufficient evidence.

But he knew that Rukmini Devi's enemies were on the watch and would take steps to see that a charge was preferred. The Sub-Inspector seemed to be anxious to secure a conviction, though he was guilty of some stupidity which he tried to cover up by making false statements in his evidence at the trial. On the other hand, Rukmini Devi showed a bold front. She indignantly denied that there was the slightest ground for the aspersions sought to be cast upon her honour. She denied that she had given any special instructions to Bhagwati, beyond telling him to carry out his ordinary duty of sleeping near the entrance, in order to give an immediate alarm in the event of an attack by dacoits. She said that she was equally unable to account for his mysterious disappearance.

If her servants chose to murder one another, she could not prevent it and it was no business of hers. Her local enemies had often vowed vengeance for their defeat and they were, in all probability, the real culprits of the crime, which they were trying to fix upon her.

Eventually, it was decided to make Jhoku an approver and to run a case based on his evidence, relying on the various items of corroboration provided by the finding of the remains – the shoes in the possession of Jhoku, the fact that Jhoku was able to identify the sack and Bishan Singh's dagger which had been used for the crime, the secret visits of Bishan Singh and his amorous correspondence. Rukmini Devi and her two servants, Raja Ram and Sundar, were eventually put upon their trial.

The case was in many ways an exceptional one and attracted a good deal of attention. In the end, of course, everything turned on the amount of credence to be given to the story told by Jhoku. He might have been put upon his trial himself. His confession did not go the length of implicating him in the actual murder. There is no such thing in the Indian Penal Code as an 'accessory after the fact'. But it is a crime to do any act with a view to remove or conceal the traces of a crime and there was no question as to Jhoku, on his own story, having aided in concealing the corpse.

•

There was enough to hang the accused, if Jhoku were to be believed.

In the majority of criminal trials, the judge is free to take a view of his own and to accept the evidence of an accomplice, if he is satisfied of its truth. Jhoku's story might have been accepted if the case was otherwise perfectly straightforward. But it was not. And it was here that the Sub-Inspector, by a foolish lack of candour, himself created difficulties for the prosecution.

Having decided to turn Jhoku into an approver, he also decided to hide him. In this, he was right. Jhoku, as a witness, could be easily tampered with, and he might easily be brought during the interval which had to elapse before the trial. So, he was sent off to some distant village to stay with a family until he was needed. Who these people really were, was never properly explained, but Jhoku was certainly not a free-agent. The cat was let out of the bag during his cross-examination at the trial.

When he was asked about his residence, he became shifty and showed the sort of nervous hesitation which generally shows that a witness is trying to conceal something. In the effort to steer between the truth and what he had been coached to say, he became almost incoherent. Either he did not know, or had been forbidden to say, where he had been living. It appeared from what he said that the wife of the head of the family where he stayed was an aunt of someone, but whether she was the aunt of Jhoku or the sub-inspector, was not clear. He had gone off by train in the company of a constable. This was a reasonable precaution for the sake of safe custody of a critical witness in a murder case. But the constable's movements were mysterious and he appeared to have left the train at some intermediate station. But where this happened, and how Jhoku eventually reached his destination, were shrouded in mystery.

•

When the Sub-Inspector came to give his evidence, the facts about this side issue became still more bewildering. He professed to know nothing about the place where Jhoku had gone. The impression which he tried to convey to the court was that some member of Jhoku's family had undertaken to look after him, and had asked that a constable should be allowed to travel with him for safety. This incident was typical of the way in which experienced members of the police force in charge of a case will go out of their way to create unnecessary difficulties. There was absolutely no reason why the Sub-Inspector should not take steps to have Jhoku protected from interference till after the trial. It is often done, and there was no reason why he should not say so in court, and instead cover it up.

One can only suppose that they have been, from time to time, so severely criticised or discredited by a sceptical tribunal for telling the truth that they occasionally seek refuge in subterfuge, imagining that they ought to hide something which has really very little importance. The consequence is not infrequently, as it was in this case, just the opposite of what they expect. Nothing is more calculated to make a trial court suspicious, especially in a criminal case where the evidence is not very strong, than an indication that the investigation officer is not telling the truth.

Once there appears to be anything not quite straight about the investigation, the judge begins to be sceptical about the evidence on which he is asked to convict. There is a constant disposition, especially amongst judges, to find fault with the methods of the police. For this, there is often only too much reason. So that when the judge trying the case begins to distrust the investigation, he becomes particularly astute in finding points of criticism and reasons for doubt about the positive portions of the case presented on behalf of the prosecution. Whatever would have been the result of the charge against Rukmini Devi, it is quite certain that the foolish conduct of the Sub-Inspector about the custody of Jhoku was sufficient in itself to raise serious doubts in the mind of any tribunal as to whether the main story could be accepted.

•

Bishan Singh was called for the defence, and his evidence was a complete denial of the alleged intrigue between him and Rukmini Devi, upon which the prosecution relied. Bishan Singh admitted the authorship of the letters, but denied that he had ever written to Rukmini Devi. He also denied the night visits to the house. He declared that he had had a mild flirtation with Rukmini Devi, who was also carrying on with a friend of his. He had sent her the verses at her request, to enable her to copy them or make what use of them she pleased with respect to her real admirer. It was pointed out to him that the reference to the horse contained a hidden suggestion that the animal would require looking after when he paid his visit to the house. The other parts of the letter indicated that a messenger was to be sent to his place. But he replied that the love letters were addressed personally to Rukmini Devi, more by way of a joke than anything else and they were intended only to make her believe that he was really in love with her and no more.

His explanations failed to carry conviction, but in the face of his evidence, it was impossible to say that the allegation of the intrigue was established. In the end, the Sessions Judge wrote a long judgment indicating that at the back of his mind, there was a shrewd suspicion that the story told by Jhoku was not far from the actual truth. But he came to the conclusion that the case was not proved to his satisfaction and that the accused were entitled to the benefit of the doubt.

This was the view generally taken by those concerned in the case, and no further light was ever thrown on the fate of Bhagwati. But, there were undoubtedly many servants in the employment of Rukmini Devi, and others living in the village, who could have told a good deal more if they had chosen to open their mouths.

6

Baalu's Tragedy

In the 1850s, some princely states to the south of Bombay Presidency had a thriving flesh market. There was a constant demand for young women, particularly among the members of the ruling class and higher aristocracy. Even the trading community, which had grown prosperous due to proximity to the Arabian Sea as well as to the city of Bombay, had caught up with the fashion. The suppliers of these young women had powerful connections in these princely states. Some even ventured into kidnapping girls and women from the adjacent British territory.

Unlike policing in the regions under direct rule of the East India Company, which was mostly in direct contact with police of other British Indian territory, policing in the native princely states was a different ball game. Few had any formal structure of police organization and still fewer would cooperate with police of the British India territory. Apprehending criminals in princely states, especially those who were not on friendly terms with the East India Company, was a herculean task.

•

Baalu was a fine young man in his early twenties, who always wanted to make it big. He did not want to spend his life in his village tilling the small piece of land which his forefathers had been cultivating since anyone could remember. He wanted to go out and see that fantastic city everyone talked so highly about – Bombay. And the sea. He had never seen sea in his life. In fact, he had never stepped beyond his neighbouring village, from which his wife Meera belonged. It had been nearly three years since he had got married. He always wanted to go to Bombay. Nothing much was happening in his life in the village anyway.

It was few days before the Ganpati festival. Baalu was elated when he came to know that Raghu, a distant cousin of his wife, was coming home. Raghu was a water-carrier, *Jalvahak*, in the Great Indian Peninsular (GIP) Railway and was posted near Bombay. Baalu's father-in-law had promised him that he would convince Raghu to find a job for Baalu in the GIP Railway as well.

Baalu prepared for this rendezvous with Raghu excitedly. On the appointed day, he put on his best clothes and mannerisms. To impress Raghu, he even managed to learn a few English words – 'Yes sir', 'no sir' and 'thank you sir'. And impress he did. Raghu was only too glad to help out young Baalu and asked him to accompany back to his place of duty after his leave was over. There, he would arrange a meeting with bada sahib and Raghu was confident that Baalu would find a job.

Mr Smith, the section engineer in the GIP Railway posted in south Bombay division, was an affable man. He could always find some use for a fine village young man. Baalu was immediately taken into services as a bearer on probation. Within six months, as fate would have it, a vacancy arose due to death by natural course of the *durban*, or the gatekeeper, and Baalu took that place.

His wife Meera was staying back at his village house, taking care of his ageing parents. Baalu, as a devoted son and caring husband, regularly remitted small sums for his parents and wife's expenses. Occasionally, he received letters from his wife written by the village accountant, the Kulkarni. It was a happy life. She would write how proud she was of him and would remind him to do his duty diligently and always guard against carelessness or complacency, and keep bada sahib pleased with his hard work.

Years passed by. On one occasion, six months passed without Baalu having received any letter from his wife or any news about her. Worried, he wrote a letter to the village headman, the local Patel, requesting him to visit his house and give him news about his ailing parents and other family members. The reply from Patel was quick and short. His parents had been doing alright and his wife had gone to her parent's place about a fortnight ago, due to the death of a close relative.

Baalu didn't quite like this. In his absence, his wife should be taking care of his parents. How could she just go to her parents' place for so many days? He was not sure if this was the first time such a thing had happened. He immediately applied for a leave, and after obtaining the leave with some difficulty, left for his village forthwith. When Baalu reached home, his wife had been gone for over thirty-five days. He took permission from his father to go his in-laws' place to fetch her He set off the very next morning. To his utter shock, he found that his wife had never been to her parents' place!

Further inquiry revealed that the Patel of his village was a man of extremely dubious character, and recently, he had got involved with certain nobles of the princely states to the south of Bombay Presidency. In fact, one of the nobles had visited Patel's house and had been entertained for few days, about the same time his wife had left. Further investigation revealed that it was the Patel himself who had informed his parents about the death of a close relative in Meera's family and Patel had escorted Meera to her parent's village.

Baalu was filled with sudden rage and immediately rushed to Patel's house. He shouted at Patel, calling him a cheat and a liar. He demanded to know the whereabouts of his wife. But Patel did not lose his composure or raise his voice. He simply reiterated what he had already written to Baalu earlier. But when Baalu informed him that his wife had never reached her parent's place, Patel got a little agitated. He claimed that he had escorted his wife till the main crossing, or the *chouraha* of her village, as he had other business with another acquaintance in that village. He also agreed to go to Meera's village next morning and together, they would enquire her whereabouts.

•

The two villages were a few miles only. But the way to that village ran through some very wild country and wooded ravines. A small stream ran parallel to the path to the next village which, except during the dry months of summer, had knee-deep water. Next morning, it was the Patel who reached Baalu's house at day break to take him to his wife's parental home. His demeanour betrayed any suspicion anyone had regarding any foul play on his part. Soon, the two were on their way to the next village, chatting like two friends do.

Patel returned in the evening and told Baalu' parents that having met his wife, Baalu took the train to Bombay to return to his place of work along with his wife. His details were plausible enough. Everyone heaved a sigh of relief as they learnt that Baalu was finally united with his wife. Even Baalu's parents cheered up, having learnt about the well-being of their daughter-in-law. Patel was offered warm tea as a humble offering of gratitude. No foul play was ever suspected.

•

A few months later, local herdsmen discovered a hidden human skeleton buried under the bed of the rivulet, which had almost dried up by then. The skull of the skeleton was fractured in pieces. Soon, a sizeable crowd gathered to see the skeleton. One of the neighbours identified the fractured front tooth of the skeleton and Baalu's parents were summoned. His mother, on the basis of the torn rags on the skeleton, identified it to be that of her son. She also identified the fractured front teeth. They were alarmed to see it. Unable to make sense of the whole thing, they decided to summon the police.

Soon, Salman was informed about this case. Since, he had gained a lot of prominence in the eyes of his superior officers due to his outstanding work; they decided to make him the lead.

He conducted a thorough research. As per his analysis, suspicion immediately fell on the Patel as he was the last person seen in company of the deceased. The Patel stoutly denied his guilt, but soon, his seemingly plausible story that he had narrated on the fateful day he had left along with Baalu and returned alone, was found to be false.

The Patel and Baalu had never gone to Meera's house on that day. Police investigation further revealed that about the time Meera had disappeared, when a noble from the southern princely state was entertained at the Patel's house, the Patel had suddenly become flush with cash. He suddenly bought cattle, paid off all his debts from the local money lender and bought more land.

When questioned about the sudden wealth, the Patel refused to divulge. He was arrested and produced before the magistrate, who promptly remanded him to custody. An information about Baalu's murder was sent to GIP Railway and upon interference from the bada sahib Mr Smith, detectives from Bombay were sent to his village. Although Patel's involvement was amply clear and the identity of the noble of the southern princely state who had visited the Patel at the time of disappearance of Baalu's wife was established, the problem remained in his apprehension and interrogation.

Again, with the interference of Mr Smith, the political agent in charge of the princely state, used his good offices to pressurise the Nawab of the native princely state to allow the arrest of the noble. Upon arrest, the noble was brought to Bombay and was produced before the magistrate. The detectives requested for six days police custody of the noble to allow them to locate Baalu's wife, which the magistrate granted. Finally, it was found that Baalu's wife was alive and living as one of the concubines of Nawab's own uncle. After much interference from the political agent, Baalu's wife was finally recovered by the detectives.

•

Meera revealed how the Patel had come to her at Baalu's house, giving false information of death of a close relative at her parent's place. She further narrated how the Patel escorted her out of the village and as soon as they were out of Baalu's village, he got her abducted by the noble's men. The noble, very close to the uncle of the Nawab, was into business of abducting and selling young women. Within a week, Meera found herself as one of the concubines of Nawab's uncle. It was a guarded palace and there was no chance of escape. Any women who had attempted to escape were severely beaten up.

The detectives wanted to arrest Nawab's uncle, but even the political agent expressed his helplessness in getting this done. So, the police had to be content with the two arrests that they had already made – the Patel and the noble. It came out in the investigation that the Patel was paid three hundred rupees by the noble for pointing out and helping in the abduction of Baalu's wife. Patel, on his part, had counted on Baalu staying away till enough time elapsed for it to be rumoured that Baalu's wife had ran off with someone on her own accord. Baalu's immediate return and his pertinacity had driven the Patel to desperation.

So, on the fateful day, when the Patel and Baalu were going to Meera's village through the forested road, the Patel first tried to offer a hundred rupees to Baalu to make him forget Meera. He even tried to convince Baalu that because now he was working in the GIP Railway, he could easily find a more beautiful wife who would bring richer dowry. But seeing Baalu not convinced, the Patel knocked him on the head at the first opportunity. Multiple injuries on the head and a quick burial beneath the running rivulet followed.

The trial court found both the Patel and the noble guilty of abduction, and the Patel guilty of murder. The noble was sentenced to ten years rigorous imprisonment while the Patel was to be hanged. Nawab's court presented all sort of difficulties during the trial of the case. Not a single reliable witness could be ascertained from the Nawab's state. The high court upheld the punishment awarded to the Patel, but reversed the conviction of the noble man.

As it so happened, the same native princely state, by the turn of political events, was to be merged with Bombay presidency, following the administrative changes post-1857. Among other things, it resulted in release of over two hundred women from the palace of Nawab's uncle, many of whom were abducted from British India territory, while several brought as slaves from as far as Zanzibar.

7

The Sacrifice of a Child

On 11 November 1912, Ram Saran made his appearance at the local thana in a state of inexpressible grief. He reported the sudden and mysterious disappearance of his little boy, Sohan. He had seen him alive at around 7 a.m.

During those days, the murder of little children in villages occurred with distressing frequency, and was generally due to one of the two reasons – either because of the enmity between the mother and some other female relative or a female neighbour, in which case it may happen to a mere infant, however young; or due to the greed of some male villager, who, having lured the child away from home, will throw it into a well, after stripping it of the cheap silver ornaments which parents persisted in putting upon their children of either sex.

But in the case of Sohan, his mother had no enemy who would want to inflict such an injury upon her. And, as he was only two years old, he was too young to be wearing the usual adornments. Ram Saran and his friends had already made an exhaustive search everywhere in the village as well as the surrounding fields, without discovering any clue. He had no suggestion to make by way of explanation of his loss, and his report at the police station was not likely to lead to anything.

When Salman heard about the Ram Saran's loss, he was deeply moved. He always had a strong affinity towards young children. He could fathom the sorrow of the grieving parent and decided to delve deeper to crack the tricky case.

No 'cognizable' offence was made out against anyone upon which the police could act, and the SHO usually did not send out search parties for the benefit of private individuals, unless his duties required him to take up the investigation of a definite allegation of a crime. Kidnapping would be a 'cognizable' offence, but Ram Saran was not in a position to make a charge against anyone. All he could say was that the infant, while toddling about with other children, was believed to have been led off by some young girl, but as for her name or identity, the other children were not able to give any information.

•

Ram Saran next saw his infant boy on the evening of 13 November, at the same police station. He had received a mysterious hint from a villager, who was unable to say where he had got the precise information from. He was told that a child, who was probably his missing son, had been taken there. The station was several miles away from Ram Saran's village and the child's conveyance there, instead of to his home, was also mysterious.

At the police station, Ram Saran found his son in a pitiable condition, with ghastly wounds around his thigh. The manner in which the child was recovered was again mysterious. A villager named Lakhan had brought the child to the thana, accompanied by another villager named Mathura Prasad.

Lakhan had found the child in a *nallah* or ditch, close to the village. The village was a large one. He said that he had been attracted to the spot by hearing a child's cry while he was working in a nearby field. He had told Mathura Prasad, who was also working with him, and the two together had gone in the direction from which the child's cry was coming. There, they found the child. Interestingly, there were others also working in the same field, or adjoining ones, but no one except Lakhan heard any cry. Lakhan's version of the narrative appeared a little skewed as a deserted child would not lie out in a ditch for very long without making a noise. It was quite certain that it had been kept or placed there only a short time before its cry was heard. The strong probability was that Lakhan knew perfectly well that the child was there, even if he had not put it there himself.

•

For a long time after that, Lakhan and Mathura Prasad were under the suspicious gaze of the villagers. The villagers suspected them of knowing a great deal more about the recovery of the child than they had conveyed to the police. They must have known that Ram Saran's son was missing, because Ram Saran had publicly offered a reward for anyone who helped find his son – an unusual event in a village, which was certain to attract general notice of every villager. They must, therefore, have had some special reason for carrying the child off on a long journey to the thana.

The duo said they did not know whose child it was, or what they ought to do with it. Moreover, the child seemed in a pitiable state and they feared that it might die, so they thought it best to deposit it in the local police station. The child was immediately taken from the police station to the hospital. The child was still wearing the same clothes which he had worn on the day he had disappeared and there was no trace of bloodstains upon them.

When the wounds were examined at the hospital, they were found to be large and irregular. The flesh had been actually cut away, exposing the whole of the front and half of the back aspects of the right thigh. Another wound was found on the abdomen. All these wounds appeared to have been deliberately cut with a sharp knife. A feeble attempt, originally suggested by the local doctor who somehow was not very bright, was made to show that the wounds had been caused by the bites of animals. This would be quite likely to happen if the body had been laid in the nallah for any length of time, especially for one whole night. But it would, on the other hand, be almost impossible that the two-year-old child could have survived the exposure and the attacks of wild animals combined. Moreover, the clean appearance of the other parts of the body and of the clothes when the child was found, was all against the theory of animal bite.

•

The doctor was certain that the wounds were at least twenty-four hours old. They were dry and crusted with dust, which must have been carefully sprinkled, either to staunch the blood or for healing purposes. Soil is often used by villagers with both objects. But, the wounds had been otherwise shockingly neglected. After lingering for about a week, the child died of blood poisoning and exhaustion.

Ram Saran was stricken with grief. It was his only son and he was inconsolable. He openly declared his determination not to rest until he had discovered the ones responsible for the death of his only child. The belief eventually entertained in the village was that the child had been treacherously kidnapped and used for sacrifice.

It is a curious feature of village life how these rumours gain currency, by a gradual though steady growth. They also stick around for long. Though sometimes ludicrously false, they are more often absolutely right. It seemed as though some women must have been at the bottom of this persistent rumour. During the child's illness in the hospital, while it hung between life and death, a number of women visited Ram Saran's house to ask how the child was getting on.

Amongst these sympathetic callers, Ram Saran's wife noticed one strange woman, who not only came regularly every day, but who seemed to be particularly pressing and earnest in her inquiries. The wife reported this to her husband, but beyond saying that one day the truth would be known, he did nothing. He did not even mention it to the police until the following January, for reasons of their own, they had begun making intensive investigation into the mystery. And then, the strange woman could not be found. But with a praise worthy persistence, the police officials produced woman after woman to see if Ram Saran's wife could identify the stranger that she suspected.

•

Their patience was rewarded. Towards the end of January, the police brought with them one Musammat Laraiti, and Ram Saran's wife recognised her. Laraiti seemed to have nothing to hide or to fear. She readily agreed that she was the woman who had been making visits to inquire about the child. She was a *nain*, or member of the barber caste, and she had been in the habit of doing odd jobs such as shampooing and running errands for a well-to-do lady, whom she knew only as the sister-in-law of Musammat Chironji, the wife of the zamindar who lived in a large house on the outskirts of the village.

She said that she had been sent every day by Musammat

Chironji to make inquiries about the child's health. She then told the police that she had called at the zamindar's house one afternoon, about three months earlier, and had seen a strange child in the *angan* (inner quadrangular court of the dwelling). That day, she had been told to go away. This was shortly before she had been sent to inquire about the child. She gave the police certain other information, and told them that she had always understood that the child she had seen in the angan was the same child as the one she had been sent to inquire after, and which had died. Also that Musammat Chironji had told her nothing, and had impressed upon her the necessity of preserving absolute secrecy. She told the police that she had talked the matter over with a woman named Chutkia, who was also employed at the house.

This was quite enough to account for the village rumours. Musammat Chutkia was then unearthed by the police. She was a *kaharin* of the bearer caste, and used to draw water for Musammat Chironji's household. She had more important information to give. She informed how she had seen Dwarka Prasad, Lakhan's son who had found the child of about two years of age in the nallah and brought it into the house one morning. She had been ordered to prepare and clean a square piece of ground in the courtyard, and to bring a pitcher of water. She also said that she was at the house just before the time when she understood some ceremony was to be performed. She had seen Musammat Chironji and her husband Mahesh Rai, a certain *sadhu* or ascetic named Krishna Rao, Mathura Prasad, Dwarka Prasad, and another man named Ram Narain – all assembled together, probably about to perform some religious ceremony. The next day, she had seen what she believed to be the same child, because there was no infant belonging to the household, lying on a cot, covered up to its neck with a white cloth on which there were bloodstains. The child was crying, and seemed to be in a state of semi-consciousness. She had heard two days after that the child of Ram Saran had been found the previous evening, with serious cut injuries.

•

All this appeared to create a circumstantial case against Musammat Chironji and her friends for having kidnapped the child. But there were links still missing and the police were on a case of murder – which was a very different matter from the earlier reported case of a missing child. There was ground for trying whether anything further could be extracted from those who had already been named, either by frightening them or by interrogating them. They were the last persons to have been seen with the child before it was discovered in the nallah. But the police did not know what had really happened and could not form an opinion with sufficient confidence to attempt to bluff Musammat Chironji and her friends.

Musammat Chironji was, to some extent, educated and would certainly have been carefully coached and she might stubbornly refuse to answer questions. And if the police happened to show by what they said how little they knew, they would inspire confidence rather than fear and destroy all hope of obtaining any useful information from this line of inquiry. They decided upon a bold course and arrested Krishna Rao, the sadhu. It is not clear why they took this step at this stage. But the investigation was being directed by the European Superintendent of Police, in consultation with the district magistrate or collector. Someone had been communicating with the latter and had put pressure upon him to intervene in an endeavour to solve the mystery. When such a thing happened, a matter was usually not dropped easily.

It is worth noting that there is all the difference in the world between an investigation conducted by an ordinary Sub-Inspector at the instance of a local complainant, and one in which the district magistrate is interested, and which the Superintendent of Police is personally supervising and directing step by step. In the latter case, there may not always be the same degree of subtle undermining and of those shrewd methods of patient diplomacy in which the local police excel in their dealings with the timorous villager. But there is more initiative, decision making, and occasionally bold and rapid action which leads to big results.

It was probably thought, and not without justification as subsequent events showed, that Krishna Rao would become nervous and be anxious to try and save his own skin by volunteering information. It may have been thought that the sadhu's arrest would strike terror in the hearts of the members of Musammat Chironji's family and induce some of them to make disclosures. But whatever hopes had been formed by the authorities, their bold stroke failed. Krishna Rao, while acknowledging that he was the family priest, stoutly denied all knowledge of the presence of any infant in the house. He said that he had not been present at any unusual proceeding or any meeting such as had been described by Musammat Chutkia.

•

Days passed, and several villagers also came forward with vague statements and suggestions. Mostly, only hearsay was forthcoming and the police could get hold of nothing of evident value. But suddenly, a strange thing happened. Krishna Rao fell into the hands of the police in another police station, on a charge of highway robbery. He had found that the village was getting too hot for him. Curiosity was not dying down as he had hoped. Suspicion was still attached to him and, whether his conscience smote him, his stock was falling and he decided to try a change of air and a new scope for his activities. So, he set out on foot to a distant and well-known resort of pilgrims, in company with a *sahukar* (money-lender). Later, he seized the opportunity by taking the unfortunate sahukar unawares, relieving him of some valuable ornaments which he was carrying with him in the hope of doing some profitable business in the place of pilgrimage.

The high hopes which the sahukar had undoubtedly formed of promoting his spiritual welfare by associating himself with the holy man were disappointed, but he succeeded in getting the police to arrest his treacherous companion. While in custody for the robbery, the sadhu fell into the police trap. He was informed by the SHO of the new thana where he was in police custody that the game was up and that his confederates in the child kidnapping and murder case had confessed the whole story, although it was not true and the Station House Officer was just taking his chances. The holy man thereupon remarked that he might as well do so too. And he did.

Krishna Rao narrated the entire episode without much fuss. His story was as follows:

> Musammat Chironji was much troubled because she had borne no son to her husband, who felt the matter keenly. Apart from the strong wish of every person to leave a son behind to perform the funeral rites and to do worship for the good of his departed soul, it was important in connection with the family inheritance. Musammat Chironji was afraid that she might be supplanted by her husband taking another young wife. Mahesh Rai and his mother had summoned Krishna Rao on several occasions to consult him. A learned man who was in the habit of

visiting him and doing puja but whose name he did not disclose, had told them that Musammat Chironji's sterility could be cured if she ate the warm and reeking flesh of a living child and drank its blood. This was a palpable falsehood so far as it related to the authorship of the idea. For it was certain that the family priest would not allow his authority with the household to be shaken by another taking his place as confidant and counsellor.

Eventually, the parents had decided to make the experiment and to procure a child. He was invited to the house, where he met Mahesh Rai and his mother, Musammat Chironji, Mathura Prasad, Dwarka Prasad and Ram Narain. A child was already lying there unconscious, having been intoxicated with bhang. He was asked to perform puja, or worship and the ground was plastered with cow-dung for the purpose. The child was placed inside the plastered square and Krishna performed the ceremony. Then, having put a sacred mark on the forehead of the child, he withdrew from the square and sat apart.

The criminal acts were then performed by two of the party, whom he was unable to identify, but upon whom he endeavoured in his detailed account to throw the blame. They put the child in the centre of the group. Each of them cut a piece of flesh from the thigh and with fresh cuts drew blood from below the ribs. One of them wrote a magic square, on the ground with the blood, which had been drained into a brass pot and was to be drunk by the childless woman. Krishna Rao, seeing the child wrapped in white and hearing an order given that it was to be removed, took his departure. The medical details of the act and its possible consequences, neither of which he could have prevented, did not concern him. He had been called simply to perform the puja. He noticed that the child was crying and gasping when he left, but he did not know whose it was or how it had been obtained. He said that it was no business of his to inquire. He added that the husband was never a willing party to the ceremony and had protested, but was powerless against the determined fanaticism of his women-folk. It was very difficult to say how much of this statement was true and how much was designed to save himself. This is constantly one of the chief difficulties of a criminal case in which there are several accused and one confesses to a subordinate part in order to throw the chief blame on to the others.

•

The case was an exceptional one. Not only on account of the revolting and pathetic circumstances and the unsatisfactory result of the trial, but also because there was no trace in the history of the province, nor in any of the historical writings on human sacrifice, of a similar act performed on the body of a living child for such a purpose. Although, in one sense, it may be treated as a human sacrifice, one must accept the view that neither Musammat Chironji nor any of those who took part in it desired to take the child's life. Short of having a medical man in attendance, they seemed to have done all in their power without courting discovery, to give the child a chance of recovery.

Musammat Chironji showed her finer feelings of concern by sending daily, at what she must have known to be the risk of detection, to inquire after the child's health. In the eyes of the law, they must be taken to have contemplated and intended the natural and probable consequences of their act, and all were therefore guilty of murder.

But, it must also be taken for granted that their actions were under the influence of the sadhu and in implicit belief in the sanction conferred by his traditional authority as family priest. Also, that the sadhu himself performed the operation upon the child. It is inconceivable that he would have allowed anyone else to usurp his authority in such a matter. He knew quite well that he was defying the law. He was probably prepared to accept such consequences as fate might have in store for him. Having once started, he could not turn back. His authority with the family, from whom in the past he had probably derived his main source of livelihood, would be gone for ever and his influence with others, who looked to him as their spiritual guide, would decline with it.

Many of those who follow this calling are men of exemplary life and character, and are students, if not teachers of morality, and men of much learning and simplicity. But even amongst the really devout, there are few upon whom the promptings of pride and self-importance operate more powerfully than the prickings of conscience. Such people will descend to any level which they think will do violence to the halo of sanctity with which they surround themselves.

•

Krishna Rao betrayed his contemptible character in his escape from the village, his robbery of the sahukar and in his final feeble effort to save himself at the expense of the others by denying his real share in the counselling and abetting of the murderous crime. He did not have the moral courage to rely upon the traditional tenets and beliefs which led him to recommend what was done. He provided no material from which any opinion can be formed as to the source from which he derived the idea.

It is correct to suppose that the death of Sohan was not intended and the elements of true sacrifice was lacking. If Krishna had frankly admitted that the sacrifice of the child was what he believed to be necessary, one would have been disposed to take a more merciful view of his conduct. But on this part of the case, his confession affected complete indifference, and produced no more than an impotent negative and a denial of personal participation.

•

In the present case, the accused were thus, put on their trial simply for murder. Krishna Rao's statement was recorded before a magistrate as a confession. It was enough to hang him, corroborated, by what the female servants had said.

Mahesh Rai, the husband, confirmed what Krishna had said about him and offered to give evidence. It was cowardly of him to desert his wife in this fashion. Apparently, the police believed his account of himself. They thought that his statement might be accepted by the session court, and that he would be acquitted, preferred to strengthen the case by making him a witness rather than a subordinate accused on a charge of aiding and abetting.

When he found that he had been caught in a trap, Krishna Rao took the usual course of retracting his confession. This did not seriously affect the case for the prosecution because it is one of the peculiarities of the law of evidence in India that the confession of a co-accused may be 'taken into account' against the others, even though it has been retracted. He did not take the usual course of saying that he had been tortured by the police and tutored to make a false statement. He quite frankly said that the statement had been obtained from him by the false representation that the others had confessed and it was a false one.

•

There was never the slightest doubt about the guilt of Krishna Rao. With regard to the other accused, Dwarka Prasad, the son of Lakhan, who found Sohan in the ditch, was seen by Musammat Chutkia to bring the child into the house. Mathura Prasad was the only person with Lakhan at the time and they both went to the thana with the child. It was established that Dwarka did the kidnapping, and that Mathura Prasad and Lakhan took the child away after the operation and pretended to find it. Lakhan was probably brought in because his son was already involved and he would almost certainly decline to do the finding unless he had a witness with him. Krishna Rao and Musammat Chironji were convicted but Dwarka Prasad, Mathura Prasad and Ram Narain were acquitted. Yet, if the truth of the story as a whole was established, there seemed no reason for rejecting the independent evidence of Musammat Chutkia, confirmed as it was by Krishna's confession.

•

An appeal against these acquittals was made to the High Court, but was rejected. On the whole, the three must be accounted fortunate to have escaped without punishment. The sadhu and Chironji were sentenced to transportation for life.

8

The Mystery of the Plough

The answer to the question of Madhava Narayan's death depended almost entirely upon whether he was really ploughing his field in the early hours of the fateful October morning. The mystery had never been solved.

There were at least four persons who knew the truth, but to add to the woes of Salman, the investigating officer, nobody knew who these four persons were. The way in which old Madhava Narayan met his end was either a double-bluff – an attempt by the murderer to frame his enemy for the crime which had almost succeeded, or a daylight murder in the open fields duly proved by eye-witnesses. But no one knew which it was, except the privileged four. It was like a neat judicial puzzle, despite the fact that the circumstances were simple and ordinary enough.

•

Madhava Narayan was a cultivator in the village of Phulwari. He was around sixty-five years of age and lived with Musammat[2]

2. Musammat – Wilson's Glossary defines the term as a title prefixed in Hindustan to the names of respectable women in public documents and judicial proceedings. [H H Wilson's Glossary of Judicial & Revenue Terms by Asia Law House]

Ramdulari, his nephew's widow and her two young boys. He was himself childless, his wife having died seven years ago without any child. Many in the village believed Madhava Narayan to be impotent. At the time of Madhava Narayan's death, Ramdulari was expecting another child, although her husband had been dead nearly ten years. She alleged that the father was Madhava Narayan, but she was the only one who said so. Nobody believed it.

Madhava Narayan was an occupancy tenant of an influential zamindar named Amar Singh, who was also accused of his murder. There was no love lost between the two.

It is popularly known that tenants in Indian villages are divided into two classes. A large proportion of them possessed a right of permanent and hereditary occupancy in the land so long as they paid their rent regularly. The amount of rent depended on local custom, not on competition. In some cases, they were entitled to hold at permanently fixed rates, and their right was heritable and transferable. In other cases, the rent could only be enhanced on certain grounds specified by law. Such tenants could only be ousted by a decree of court on proof of non-payment of rent, and without a decree of court, the landlord could not obtain a higher rent. Cultivators of this category were, in fact, co-sharers in the land, possessing limited rights of property. A tenant who, by himself or his ancestors, had held during twelve years uninterrupted occupation of the land acquired a permanent right of occupancy. Cultivators of this class were usually far better off than those who had no such privileges. They had more cattle, better houses, better clothes and larger areas of land. Below this class came the non-occupancy tenant, who had agreed to pay an enhanced rent but had no security of tenure.

If Madhava Narayan could survive until one of Ramdulari's boys took a genuine share in the cultivation of the holding of about two hundred acres, the tenancy could be continued after his death. Otherwise, there was a risk that it would lapse and revert to the zamindar, Amar Singh. Which is why in this case, the zamindar had a distinct interest in Madhava Narayan's demise. Moreover, a few months ago, Madhava Narayan had brought a false charge against Amar Singh, of having damaged his crops. This had been dismissed by the local magistrate, after which the mutual soreness had intensified.

It so happened that only a few days before Madhava Narayan met his violent end, Amar Singh had begun proceedings against him for having falsely and maliciously prosecuted this unfounded charge. This increased the mystery of the murder. Unless he was arranging a piece of what is called *peshbandi*, or the preparation of an argument in advance to meet an anticipated emergency (and in that case he could have done something simpler, at less cost), he would hardly have gone to the trouble and expense of bringing a civil suit against himself, if he intended to murder Madhava.

One morning, early in the month of October, Ramdulari arrived at the nearest thana, five miles away from Phulwari village. She was accompanied by Ganga Sahai, the village chaukidar, and someone called Mangat. She had come to report the murder of Madhava Narayan early that morning, by zamindar Amar Singh and his nephew Kalyan. She gave some account of the relations between the zamindar and the deceased to make the position clear. She asserted that on the previous evening, at the time of the evening meal, Amar Singh had sent a messenger to Madhava Narayan to summon him to his *baithaki* or that place in his residence where the zamindar usually sat to talk with visitors and to transact business.

On returning home, Madhava had narrated that Amar Singh had threatened him, saying that if he went to plough his field the next morning, he would be beaten on the spot. But in spite of the threat, Madhava Narayan had gone particularly early that morning, at around 3:00 a.m. He had gone alone, Ramdulari reported, taking with him his two bullocks and his plough.

Before sunrise, Girwar, a cultivator residing in another village, had come to her house and told her that he had seen Amar Singh and Kalyan beating Madhava Narayan with a lathi. He saw the old man fall down but he did not know whether he was dead. He had told her to go and see for herself. She had found Madhava Narayan lying dead with his head smashed in, after which she had come to make her report.

This report, while not lacking detail relating to the animosity existing between the two men – a topic upon which the ordinary villagers and women were extremely eloquent – gave very little detail of what she had seen at the field. It also omitted an important detail about her own movements from the time when Girwar had arrived at her house. After the clerk had taken down Ramdulari's statement, Salman and his men went straight to the field for a thorough inspection. A certain amount of ploughing had taken place, but the land was wet and in certain places almost water-logged as the result of the recent heavy rain. One furrow across the field had been ploughed, and a short length of a second.

At the spot where the ploughed portion of the second line stopped lay the dead body of Madhava Narayan. Peculiarly, the ploughing had begun from the middle. The injuries, as subsequently disclosed by the post-mortem, were peculiar too. Death had been caused by a terrible fracture of the skull. There were also two small, round, definitely punctured wounds in the head, one of which had entered the brain. Three ribs had been broken and the chest appeared as though considerable pressure had been exerted upon it. There was another punctured wound which had reached the lungs. All these punctured wounds appeared to have been inflicted by a weapon with a long, sharp point, carefully directed. It was probable that the victim was lying down when they were inflicted. The blow on the head was almost certainly delivered by a lathi when he was standing but it might have been done from behind, as per the doctor.

•

Not far from the body, Salman found a stick with a pointed blade attached to it, in shape like a rough golf club, which the deceased was said to carry with him for the purpose of scraping his plough. But, the doctor was positive that this could not have caused the punctured wounds. Moreover, no stains of blood were found on it.

With the soil in the condition after the rain, a good deal of scraping would have to be done to the plough. It was clear that the stick belonged to Madhava. It was certain that he had taken it with him for ploughing. But, it was possible for Ramdulari to have got hold of it, and either herself or in collusion with a conspirator, have placed it on the field. Close to the body, Salman found the plough, a yoke and a pair of shoes. The latter might have been anyone's, but were said to have belonged to Madhava. They were a mystery of their own.

If he was wearing his shoes when he left home, who took them off? And why? The bullocks were gone. They were neither seen, nor heard of by Salman or his team. The next day, they were reported to have been found in the village by a boy. He had found them on the day of the murder. The movements of the bullocks were somewhat mysterious. The first furrow which had been ploughed looked regular and straight. The unfinished furrow looked as though the ploughing had been done carelessly or rapidly and had been interrupted two or three times.

Further, there was no sign of the bullocks having escaped, or having made their way back to the village while yoked to the plough. No marks of any dragging of the plough were seen near the place of crime. There was a distinct impression in the soil and a patch of fresh-looking dung, which indicated that the bullocks had sat down there.

Salman presumed they must have been unyoked after the ploughing. Again, who unyoked them, and why? At what time they left the spot, which road they took, or how and when they got to the village? These were points which were never cleared. No one saw them in the course of their journey. At least no one came forward to say so, until the boy came upon them, as he said, about midday. A regular search for the bullocks was instituted during the forenoon, but the constables failed to see or hear anything about them that day.

Bullocks are heavy, slow-moving animals. Their primary instinct, when they are supposed to work, seems to be to remain stationary as long as possible. They know their master, their crib at night and their usual feeding place. Like their masters, they also suffer from the usual tropical lethargy. They generally require a stick to galvanise them into activity or anything like a brisk walk. These observations are obvious but they serve to emphasise the difficulty of believing that anyone could have found the bullocks in the village on the day of the murder, without the police becoming aware of the fact.

A search was also made for Amar Singh and his nephew, but neither of them could be found. Warrants were issued for their arrest. According to a few villagers, Amar Singh had been seen in the village that morning. He returned in a few days and gave himself up, stating that he had been absent on business, and had come back as soon as he had heard that he was wanted. He was able to prove a reliable alibi, even during the night and early morning of the crime.

The real controversy at the trial, and the mystery which still clings to the tragedy was whether Amar Singh had deliberately murdered his tenant, or whether his enemies had arranged the murder in order to implicate him in a capital charge. His presence in the village on the morning of the crime was established with either view. On the one hand, it made his actual participation in the murder physically possible. On the other hand, the ones conspiring against him could hardly have overlooked such an elementary detail as his presence in the village on the night of the crime. It was urged on his behalf that if he had taken such elaborate precautions to affect the murder of his victim at an early hour, when hardly anyone was around, the further precaution of avoiding recognition anywhere in the neighbourhood during the morning was a comparatively obvious one.

It became critical to leave aside the story told by Girwar – the alleged eye-witness to the murder. The substantial case for the defence was the old story of rivalry between two neighbouring zamindars, Amar Singh and Maharaj Singh. Applying the old principle of natural justice in criminal cases, it was the duty of the prosecution to prove their case and the defence were not called upon to show what had really happened. But, there was a good deal in the evidence which was at least consistent with the alternative suggestion.

If Musammat Ramdulari had been in the plot, and the agents of Maharaj Singh had laid wait for Madhava Narayan when he left his house in the early morning, and had then set upon him and beaten him to death, it would have been perfectly easy for them to carry the corpse to the field. They could have a little ploughing and taken the bullocks back to the village. The failure to trace a pointed weapon at the crime scene was a difficulty in the way of the prosecution. Leaving on the field the yoke and the pair of shoes looked like an attempt, though a clumsy one, to identify Madhava Narayan with the ploughing. It might have been thought necessary if the bullocks that was actually used to do the ploughing were not his. This may seem a far-fetched argument, but the presence of these articles was difficult to reconcile with any view of the case for the prosecution.

•

The case for the defence did not rest merely on these suggestions. The evidence showed that Musammat Ramdulari was on very friendly, if not intimate, terms with Maharaj Singh. Several witnesses swore at the trial to circumstances pointing in this direction. The village chaukidar said that he had seen Ramdulari visiting Maharaj's residence. They even claimed that there was an intrigue between them.

On the other hand, Ramdulari's statement that her condition was due to her relations with the deceased seemed almost incredible, for everyone in the village believed the deceased to be an impotent.

The feud between the two zamindars was proved to have been of old standing. Their fathers had been enemies before them and had fought a big partition case. Maharaj Singh would probably welcome the opportunity of involving his enemy in a criminal charge. Moreover, if there was any relation between him and Ramdulari, it brought him into close relation with all the main actors in the drama.

Ganga Sahai, the chaukidar told a remarkable tale. He said he had been called to the baithak of Maharaj Singh about dawn. As per him, it was shortly after the news of attack on Madhava Narayan reached Ramdulari. There, he found Ramdulari, Girwar and Jhankoo, the two eye-witnesses and some other persons. As per this statement, there was a conflict between the chaukidar and Jhankoo, who said that he never went to Maharaj Singh's place at all. Ganga Sahai was then asked to go to the field and look at the body, and afterwards to go on to the thana and report a case of murder against Amar Singh and his nephew. He had done so with Ramdulari and Mangat.

Now, if this were true, Ramdulari had omitted from her report the important facts that she had first visited Maharaj Singh and had afterwards gone to the field. Also, that the chaukidar and Mangat had been with her when she first saw the dead body. She, on the other hand, denied that it had happened at all. She said that she had seen no one when she went to the field. She had started alone for the thana and had come upon the chaukidar quite unexpectedly outside the village, sitting alone on a bridge. According to her, it was she who persuaded him to accompany her, which he had done without first going to see the body, though it was not much distance away. Where and why they had picked up Mangat, she did not explain.

The suggestion for the defence was that Mangat was an emissary of Maharaj Singh who had been detailed to see that Ramdulari made the proper report. According to the chaukidar, he had left Maharaj Singh's place with both of them. According to Ramdulari, she did not know Maharaj Singh, and had not been to his baithak that morning. Mangat did not confirm either of these witnesses and declined to make any statement. The chaukidar did not correct any omissions in Ramdulari's report in the thana. He said that it was her report and he refused to accept any responsibility for it, except in so far as it mentioned that the man had been murdered.

•

A further interesting point was the hour at which the deceased took his supper the evening before he was murdered. Ramdulari originally stated that Amar Singh sent for him 'at the hour of the evening meal.' Now, if the meal had been cooked and was ready at the time, it was very unlikely that Madhava Narayan would have left before eating it. It was to be remembered that the old man and the woman had to be up early next morning; the former was said to have gone to work at 3 a.m. After a long day's work, it would be a great sacrifice, especially at the invitation of an unfriendly zamindar, to abandon the evening meal and to rush off on an empty stomach.

It was more likely that Madhava Narayan ate his evening meal before he responded to his zamindar's summons. But the medical evidence showed, from the appearance of the undigested food still remaining in his stomach, that Madhava Narayan had met his death within four hours of his last meal. This suggested that he had been murdered at, or near his house, before midnight. It looked like a serious difficulty in the prosecution case. It was met by Ramdulari's statement that when Madhava Narayan returned at midnight, he repeated to her what had happened at his interview with Amar Singh, cut fodder for the animals, and then took his meal and went to bed. One can only say that it does not sound at all probable, especially for a man of his advanced age.

But the more difficult question was – did Amar Singh sent for Madhava Narayan at all? If yes, why? The soil was not really ready for ploughing. There was nothing to show that Madhava Narayan had intended to plough. But if Amar Singh intended to murder him early in the morning, he would hardly send for him and tell him not to go. It might be suggested that he hoped that Madhava Narayan would do the exact opposite. But that would make it a rather risky proceeding.

Did Madhava Narayan go to plough? Salman observed that some of the field was under water and much of it was unfit for ploughing. Evidence from the village proved that no one else had begun to plough. It was earlier in the year than the customary date for opening ploughing operations. Why was he in such a hurry to begin? And if he had to begin anyway, then why before the sun was up? Given his age, was he not likely to have taken with him the boy who could help with the bullocks or some menial assistance? This argument seemed almost overwhelming if he had indeed been threatened with a beating.

•

The local witnesses at the trial were insistent that he had not done his own ploughing for years. It was also said that he had no bullocks of his own. He had indeed sworn in the case against Amar Singh, which he lost, that he had none. The purchase of one had not even been registered by him in the previous September. But this was as near as anyone got to proving that he had two bullocks in October, or that he went to plough, except the statement of the partly discredited Musammat Ramdulari. It certainly was, if true, the oddest ploughing that ever was. On the other hand, it was never proved that he did not go.

The stage was reached when one naturally turns to the evidence of those who declared that they saw the accused committing the crime.

The circumstantial evidence leaves one in a state of hesitancy and expectation. Circumstantial evidence, it has been often said, is the most satisfactory and convincing of all, if it is sufficiently strong. Not all lawyers and textbook writers agree about this, but it is often true. Eyewitnesses are often partisan and coached; much of their evidence is inaccurate and contradictory, sometimes entirely invented. It is freely said that these details are invented by the lawyer, or *karinda* (agent) for the case.

Circumstantial evidence coming from a variety of different sources fit into their places in the larger scheme of things. It links up things in a way in which no foresight or subtle plan could have provided and forms a stable structure when complete. It enjoys superiority over eyewitnesses, but was of no avail in solving this mystery.

It rested, therefore, with those who charged Amar Singh with the murder to drive home the accusation by the direct evidence of unimpeachable witnesses and this, they failed to do. They called Girwar and Jhankoo. Both happened to be tenants of Maharaj Singh. This was a bad start. Girwar's account of what he saw was a curious one. While going to his field to see if it was ready for ploughing – a matter which was obviously so doubtful that to go at 3 a.m. was a piece of eccentricity – he heard Amar Singh abusing the deceased. He said that he was then, close to a hundred yards away. Clearly, he could not hear what was being said at that distance but he was able to distinguish who the disputants were, so it must have been nearly daylight. He made for a well about forty yards away from them. On his way to the well, he met Jhankoo. He was going to Girwar's village and asked what the matter was. As Jhankoo could both see and hear as well as Girwar, the reason for this question was obscure. Moreover, they went on to the well together and watched. All this took some time and the quarrel was already proceeding when Girwar first heard the men's voices.

•

Yet, almost at the identical moment when the two spectators arrived at the well, Amar Singh had been addressing Madhava Narayan with a foul epithet very familiar in village quarrels.

'I told you last night not to plough.' Then, turning to Kalyan, he said, 'Kalyan, beat him'. Why would he address his nephew by name when two witnesses were watching? So that there should be no mistake as to who it was?

Kalyan then, hit Madhava Narayan on the head with a lathi and Madhava Narayan fell. Thereupon Girwar, without waiting to see what else might happen, went off to the village and told Musammat Ramdulari while Jhankoo went off in the other direction towards Girwar's village. He denied the chaukidar's statement that he was at Maharaj Singh's house that morning.

No ground was shown for discrediting the chaukidar whose evidence was clear and straightforward. Girwar was unable to explain why he went directly to Ramdulari. He knew her by sight, not by name and knew that she was related to Madhava Narayan. But, he had seen nothing to lead to the belief that Madhava Narayan was dead, although Ramdulari said that he told her to go and see if he was.

•

But the most difficult part of his story was the remarkable coincidence that the first and almost only words which reached the ears of both Girwar and Jhankoo were the reference to the incident of the night before, which Ramdulari had repeated. It was strange, when one comes to think of it, this vital reference to the threat of the evening before should have been made at all. On the theory that Ramdulari had spoken the truth, the accused and his nephew were out to beat the old man, if not to kill him outright and any preliminary discussion was superfluous. Still more remarkable was that this reference to the evening's conversation should have occurred in the middle of abuse which had been going on for some time, that too at the very moment when the two eye-witnesses were within earshot.

Amar Singh and Kalyan hailed to act with dispatch if they were intent on murdering the man and to get away as soon as they could. They were unlikely to prolong the interview until spectators had time to come up. When questioned about the weapons they saw, both Girwar and Jhankoo stated that only a lathi was visible in Kalyan's hand. Was Amar Singh carrying some other weapon too?

No sharp-pointed instrument was seen. In most respects, Jhankoo agreed with Girwar's evidence, particularly in repeating the words said to have been uttered by Amar Singh. Jhankoo left the spot to continue his journey for the usual reason. He did not want to be involved in a criminal case. It did not occur to either of these bright specimens to watch the sequel. It would be asking too much of the ordinary villager to expect him to go to the rescue of the assaulted man, even though only one of the assailants was armed and though with a little management, the three of them could have over powered the two. Nor did they, while keeping at a respectful distance, think of following the assailants off the ground, back to the village and of denouncing them for a cowardly attack on a defenceless old man.

In short, their accounts were too good to be true. They heard just enough to corroborate the improbable part of Ramdulari's report and they saw all that was necessary to establish a clear case of guilt. They did not see the departure of the culprits from the scene. Kalyan departed altogether from the village and did not, like his uncle, come back again before the trial, though he probably did after the acquittal.

This was one of the most awkward points. It could not be used against Amar Singh, because Kalyan Singh was neither with him when he left the village, nor during his absence. But the acquittal of Amar Singh was the final chapter. The murderer of the old cultivator could never be traced which made it the most difficult case of Salman's career.

9

Samba - A Dog Tragedy

Salman was engrossed in his novel when the door bell rang. It was a Sunday afternoon and he was not expecting a visitor. Reluctantly, he opened the door. To his surprise, he saw Major Bowen who entered in a very exasperated state.

It had been two years since the First World War was over. The Royal British Granadiers were quartered in Danapur near Patna and their second-in-command was Major Bowen, a self-contained soldier who lived alone in one of those thatched bungalows that resembled monstrous mushrooms, bordering the racecourse.

'The Major,' as he was called by everyone, was best described by negatives. He was not married. He was not a ladies' man. Neither he was a sportsman; nor handsome, young, rich; nor even clever in general acceptance. He was not remarkable for anything except his dog.

Major Bowen and his dog, whom he had fondly named Samba, had joined Granadiers from another regiment six years ago. Though the pair was at first coldly received, they adapted themselves so admirably to their new surroundings that before long, they had gained the esteem and goodwill of both rank and file. As time went by, there arose an ill-concealed jealousy of their old corps and a disposition to ignore the fact that they had not always been part and parcel of the gallant Granadiers.

Although poor and having little besides his pay, the Major was liberal, just and generous. He had an extremely lofty standard of honour and of the value of his lightest word. He gave a good shape to the officers' mess, and though, he was strict with the youngsters, they all liked him. Inflexible as he could look on parade or in the orderly room, elsewhere he was always sympathetic to genuine causes of leave as well as helping his fellow men. He was a smart officer and a capital horseman which was another source of his popularity. He lent his horses and ponies, with ungrudging good faith, to those in his regiment who wanted to have a game of polo or race or hunt. Major Bowen did not race or hunt and rarely played polo. In fact, he was not much interested in anything. Upwards of forty, he was supremely indifferent to his dinner as well. The only thing he really cared about was his dog – a sharp, well-bred fox-terrier, with bright eyes and lemon-coloured ears, who he had named Samba.

This name was given to him in acknowledgment of his accomplishments – the agreeable manner in which he did the honours of his master's bungalow and the extraordinary care he took of him, and his property. He went around the compound early every morning, and rigorously turned out vagrants, suspicious-looking visitors to the servants' quarters, and all dogs and goats. He accompanied his master to the mess, and fetched him home, no matter how late the hour and through the rains (they are no joke in Patna). It was of no avail to tie him up at home. Not only were his heart-rending howls audible for a quarter of a mile, but on one occasion, he actually arrived under the dinner-table, chain and all, to the discomfort of the Colonel's legs, the great scandal of the mess-sergeant, and his own everlasting disgrace!

His master's friends were his friends, and took Samba quite seriously. But he drew the line at dogs. It must be admitted that his manners, to his own species, were not always nice. He had an ungentlemanly habit of suddenly sitting down and sniffing the tainted air that was a deliberate insult to any fellow dog. Many a battle was fought, many a bite was given and received. Samba was undeniably accomplished; he fetched papers and slippers, gave the paw, and in the new style on a level with his head, walked briskly on his hind legs and could strum on the piano.

•

When the Major entered Salman's house, it was uncanny that Samba was not with him. "Hope everything is fine, Major?" Salman asked curiously.

"Nothing is fine, Salman! I am doomed. Samba… my…dog…" The Major broke down. Salman rushed to the kitchen to get him a glass of water.

Major drank some water and calmed down. Salman waited for him to attain composure. After a brief pause, he said, "What happened to your dog, Major?"

Major took a deep breath and told him everything.

•

Samba was passionately fond of music and escorted his owner to the band. Rather, he escorted him almost everywhere to the club, around the barracks, the race course and even to the church. Major Bowen was not the least ashamed of his affection for his dog. It was his weak point. Even the Company's *dhobis* approached him through his favour. He was the president of the mess, and in an excellent manner, had officiated for years in that difficult and thankless office.

Once a doctor friend of the Major had to sail back to England, he requested the Major to look after his female fox-terrier in the meanwhile. From that episode, the Major got the idea of having a family for Samba.

When Samba had his first and only family, it was quite a great local event. The Major's establishment was turned completely upside down. There was racing and chasing to procure two milch goats for the use of the infants and their parent and the most elegant wadded basket was provided as a cradle. But, alas! Samba proved to be an indifferent parent. He appeared to be as hostile to his infants as he had been to others of his species. The Major had to embarrassingly make alternate arrangements for the doctor's pet and her little ones. But, before the shifting could be done, one of the neglected children pined and eventually died. It was placed in a cigar box and buried in a neat little grave under a rose-bush in the compound while its father looked on from far off, a totally uninterested spectator!

•

It was towards the end of the monsoon, when the compound was almost afloat that Major Bowen became seriously ill with malaria fever. He had been in India for seventeen years, "five years too long," the doctor declared. He must go home at once and never return to India. This was bad news for the regiment. He was dangerously ill in that lofty, bare, whitewashed bedroom in Infantry Lines. But, he would not be the first to die there. Many had perished to malarial fever before him. His friends were devoted and anxious. Samba was dedicated and distracted. He lay all day long at the foot of his cot, watching and listening, and following his slightest movement with a pair of agonized eyes. At last, there was a change and for the better. The patient was promoted into a cane lounge in the sitting room, asked to eat solids and to meet the society as represented by half the regiment.

The Major looked around his meagrely furnished little room with interested eyes. There was not a speck of dust to be seen. Everything was in its place. Samba's basket was pushed into a far corner. He had not used it for weeks. Both of them were going home, and would soon say goodbye to the steep-roofed thatched bungalow, the creaking cane chairs, the red purdahs, to the verandahs, to the neat little garden and to this regiment. Their tickets were booked. They were off in three days.

That afternoon, the Major had all his kit and personal property paraded in his sitting room, in order that the packing of his belongings should take place under his own supervision. The bearer was in attendance, and with him his slave and scapegoat, whom he called the *chhokra*. The bearer was a stolid, impassive-looking man, with a square black beard, and a somewhat sullen eye.

"Abdul," said his master, as his gaze travelled languidly from one neatly folded pile of clothes to another. From guns in cases to guns not in cases, to clocks, revolvers, watches, candlesticks the collection of ten years, parting gifts, bargains and legacies.

"You have been my servant for six years and have served me well. I have twice raised your wages and you have made a very good thing out of me. I believe I can retire and set up a *gadi*, or a shop. I am going away and never coming back. I want to give you something of mine to remember me by. You understand?" the Major said.

The bearer deliberately unfolded his arms and *salaamed* in silence.

"You may choose anything you like out of this room," continued the Major, with recklessness.

Abdul's eyes glittered curiously. It was as if a torch had suddenly illumined two inky-black pools.

"Sahib never making joke, sahib making really earnest?" Abdul asked, casting on him a glance of almost desperate eagerness. The glance was lost on his master, whose attention was fixed on a discarded gold-laced tunic and mess-jacket.

"Of course," he said to himself, "Abdul will choose them!" For gold lace is ever dear to everyone. It sells so well in the bazaar and melts down to such advantage.

"Making earnest?" Abdul repeated. The Major said irritably, "Do I ever do otherwise? Look sharp and take your choice."

"Salaam sahib," he answered, and turned quickly to where Samba was coiled up in a chair. "I take my choice of anything in this room. Then, I take the dog."

"The dog!" repeated his owner, with a half-stupefied air.

"Verily, I am fond of Samba. Samba is fond of master. The dog and I will remember the sahib together, when he is far away."

The sahib felt as if someone had suddenly plunged a knife in his heart. In Abdul's bold gaze, in Abdul's petition, he recalled the solemn (but despised) warning of a brother-officer, "This bearer of yours is a vindictive brute. You had got his son turned out of the mess as he was a drunken, thieving hound. But sleek as your bearer looks, Abdul will have it in for you yet."

And this was accomplished, when he said, "The dog and I, sahib, will remember you together."

•

Major Bowen was still desperately weak, and he had just been dealt a crushing blow. After a pause, and with a superhuman effort, he boldly confronted the two devils – the open-mouthed, gaping chhokra and the respectfully exultant bearer – and said, "*Accha*!" That is to say, "Good. It is well."

And then, he feebly waved to the pair to depart from him, for he was tired. Truly it was anything but good. It seemed the worst calamity that could have befallen him. He was alone and face to face with a terrible situation. He must either forfeit his word or his dog. Which was it to be?

In all his life, to the best of his knowledge, he had never broken his faith and now to do it to his servant, that was absolutely out of the question. But his dog, his friend, his companion with whom he never meant to part, as long as he lived! He sat erect and looked over at Samba, where he lay curled up; his expressive eyes met his master's eagerly.

His master lay back with a groan, and turned his face away from the light, a truly miserable man! His faithful friend! To have to part with him to one of the regiments would have been grief enough; but to a servant, with their unconcealed scorn of dogs! He must have been mad when he made that rash offer, but then, in justification, his common sense urged, "How was he to suppose that Abdul would choose anything but a silver watch, a gun, or the worth of fifty rupees?"

•

Major Bowen was far from being an imaginative man, but as he lay awake all night long and listened to the wild roof-cats stealing down the thatch, one mental picture stood out as distinctly as if he was looking at it. A low, squalid mud hut in a bazaar; a string bed and tied to it by a cord was Samba. Samba with thin ribs, a staring coat and misery depicted on his little face, the sport of the children and the flies, starved, forlorn, heartbroken dumbly wondering what had happened to his master and why he had so cruelly deserted him. Oh, when was he coming to fetch him?

What an insane promise! As he recalled it, he clenched his hands in intolerable agony. Why did he not offer his watch or his rifle? He would give Abdul a thousand rupees to redeem the dog, but his inner consciousness assured him that Abdul was already well-to-do. His revenge was worth more to him than money. He knew, to his cost, that Abdul had a stern, tenacious, relentless nature. At one moment, he decided to poison Abdul, or Samba, with his own hands – prussic acid was speedy. At another, he had resolved to remain in India, doctors or no doctors.

"And sacrifice your life?" breathed common sense. "Die for a dog!" True, but the dog was not a dog to him. He was his comrade, his sympathizer, his friend. Meanwhile, the object of all these mental wrestling and agonies slept the sleep of the just, innocent and ignorant. His master never closed his eyes. He saw the dawn glimmer through the bamboo chicks. He saw Abdul, the avenger, appear with his early morning tea and Abdul found him in high fever. Perhaps Abdul was not greatly surprised!

Friends and brother-officers flocked in that day, and sat with the Major. They noted with concern that he looked worse than he had done at any period of his illness. His naturally pinched face was worn and haggard to a startling degree. Moreover, in spite of the news of the high prices his horses had fetched, he was terribly down. And why? A man going home, after seventeen years in India, would be generally intolerably cheerful. They did their best to enliven him and talked incessantly of Samba.

"He is looking uncommonly fit," said young Stradbrooke, the owner of his one-time wife. "He knows he is going to England. I wonder how he will stand fourteen days at sea?"

There was a perceptible silence after this question and then, the Major said in a queer voice. “He is not going.”

“Not going?” An incredulous pause, and then someone exclaimed. “Come on, Major! You know you would just as soon leave your head behind.”

“All the same, I am leaving Samba.”

“And which of us is to have it?” cried the Adjutant. “Take notice, all, that I speak first. You won’t pass over me, sir. Samba and I were always very chummy and I want him to look after my chargers and servants, fetch my slippers, bring me home from mess and to take care of me and keep me straight.”

“I have already given it away to…” the rest of the sentence seemed to stick in the Major’s throat and his face worked painfully.

“Away to whom?” repeated young Stradbrooke.

“Say it’s to me, sir. I’ve one of the family already and Samba likes me. I know his favourite biscuits, and there are heaps of rats in my stables”.

“Given him to the bearer Abdul,” he answered, stoutly enough, though there was still a little nervous quivering of the lower lip.

If the ceiling had parted asunder and straightway tumbled down on their heads, the Major’s audience would not have been so much shocked. For a whole minute, they sat agape and then one burst out, “I say, Major, it’s a joke! You would not give him out of the regiment.”

“He is promised,” replied the Major, in a sort of husky whisper.

•

Everyone knew that the Major’s promises were a serious matter and after this answer, there ensued a long-dismayed silence. The visitors eventually turned the topic and tried to talk of other matters – the last gazette, the new regimental ribbon, of anything but of what every mind was full, Samba.

The news created quite a sensation that evening at the mess, far more than that occasioned by a newly-announced engagement, for there was an element of mystery about this topic. Why had the dog been given away?

"Major must be out of his mind," was the general verdict. "Poor old chap, to give the dog to that rascal Abdul, of all people!"

"The proper thing now, of course, is to buy the dog and keep him in the regiment. And when the Major came to his right senses, how glad he would be, dear old man!"

The Adjutant waylaid Abdul in the road, and said, curtly, "Is this true, about the dog? That your sahib has given him to you?"

Abdul salaamed. How convenient and non-committal was that gesture!

"What will you take for him?"

"I never selling my master's present," re-joined the bearer, with superb dignity.

"What does a nigger want with a dog?" demanded the officer, scornfully. "Swap him! That won't hurt your delicate sense of honour. I'll get you an old pariah out of the bazaar, and give you fifty rupees to buy him a collar!"

"I have refused today one thousand rupees for the animal," said Abdul.

"You lie, Abdul," said the officer, sternly. "Or else you have been dealing with a stark, staring madman."

"I telling true, Captain Sahib. I swear."

"Who made the offer?"

"Major".

"Great Scott! Poor dear old chap".

Then, after a moment, he finally spoke to Abdul, "Look here. Don't say a word about that offer. Come over to my quarters, and I'll give you some money. The sun has been too much for your sahib and mind you, be kind to the dog. If not, I'll come and shoot him, and thrash you within an inch of your life."

"Gentlemen Sahib never beating servants. Sahib touch me, I summon in police court, and I bring report to regimental commanding officer. Also, I going my own country, Bareilly, and I never, never selling kind master's present."

After a pause, the Adjutant added, "I know lots of sahibs in the *pultoon* (regiment) at Bareilly, and I shall get them to look out for you and the dog, Mr Abdul. You treat kind master's present well, and it will be well with you. If not, by Jove, you will find that I have got a long arm. I am a man of my word, so keep your mouth shut about the Major. Tonight, my bearer will give you ten rupees." And he walked on.

"The Major must be in a real bad shape when he gives his beloved dog to a native and wants to buy it back for a thousand rupees the next day," said Captain Young to himself.

The hour of the Major's departure arrived. He had entreated that no one would come to see him off. This request was looked upon as more of his eccentricity and not worthy of serious consideration.

Everyone thought he would get all right as soon as he was at sea and the officers who were not on duty hurried down to see the last of their popular comrade. He drove up late, looking like death, his face so withered, drawn and grey, and got out of his car, promptly followed by Abdul, carrying Samba. The steamer on river Ganges that would take him to Calcutta lay puffing and snorting at the steps. The other passengers were aboard and there was not a moment to lose.

The Major bade each and all a hurried farewell. He took leave of Samba last. It was still in Abdul's arms, and believed in his simple dog mind that his master was merely bound for one of those detestable sails up the harbour. As he offered him an eager paw, little did he guess that it was goodbye forever or that he was gazing at him for the last time. The Major descended the steps and took his place in the tender that was to convey him to the steamer. He watched the crowd of friends wildly waving handkerchiefs.

But he watched, above all, with a long, long gaze of inarticulate grief, a dark turbaned figure that stood conspicuously apart, with a small white object in his arms: watched almost breathlessly, till it faded away into one general blur.

The civilian who sat next to Major Bowen in the steamer stared at him in contemptuous astonishment. This was the first time he had seen an Englishman quit the shores of India with tears in his eyes.

10

A False Scent

The brutal and altogether unprovoked murder of Bimal Prasad was one of the glaring crimes belonging to the category of unsolved mysteries of which the annals of crime are full. Salman derived a lot of lessons from this particular investigation as it was a striking example of the way in which men who have spent their lives in the investigation of crime may lose all touch with the real solution by following a false scent too slavishly.

There is just a possibility that the Sub-Inspector who was investigating the case, was not in search of the truth. He allowed himself to become the tool of the real culprit.

The ground for entertaining this suspicion will appear later in the narrative, and the readers must draw their own conclusions. But, the case serves as a warning to honest detective officers against accepting an apparently obvious conclusion from simple, unobscured facts. The case is also a perfect instance, not only of the value of a court of appeal in criminal cases, but also of the way in which trained lawyers on both sides and also the tribunal itself, may go completely astray by overlooking an admitted fact. The bearing of it is not immediately apparent on the general issue but which, when once noticed and followed up through its implications, may alter the whole aspect of the evidence.

•

We often miss the things which are right under our noses. The history of litigation shows that it is possible for everyone in the heat of controversy to miss a point of utmost importance, which has become buried or lost in the crowd just because of being uncontroversial.

Bimal Prasad was the head of an ordinary humble family of cultivators in an outlying village. He was quite a young man, and not particularly virile. There seemed to be a strain of debility on the male side of his family. The household consisted of his young wife, Musammat Amin Kunwar; her mother, Musammat Baguli; two of his paternal aunts, Musammat Pyari and Musammat Munia, who were comparatively young; and his brother, Moti, aged eighteen, who suffered from indifferent health.

Musammat Amin Kunwar was an exceptionally beautiful and attractive young woman. There were those in the village who said that she was not too well satisfied with her husband and was quite aware of her fascination for the other male. She knew about her power of making conquests if she had the chance though there was nothing definite against her character.

On the night of the murder, the two brothers were occupying separate charpoys in the same inner room. The two aunts occupied two separate small rooms adjoining one another, each of which opened out into the courtyard where Musammat Amin Kunwar and her mother slept together on the same charpoy in the open. In a corner of the courtyard, which was only a few square feet, closed in by ordinary mud walls, was a stack of *bhusa* (hay). It was near the opening in the wall which served as the entrance and at the end farthest from the room in which the two brothers slept. The entrance was closed at night by a rough sort of door on a chain. It would not be difficult for anyone to affect an entrance noiselessly, either by inserting his hand between the door and the doorpost and removing the chain, or by climbing the wall. Cattle were tethered outside, and the house could be approached without passing either through or very close to the adjoining houses.

•

Moti's young wife was away on a long visit to her parents. Owing to the state of her husband's health, married life had very little attraction for her, and she did not get on well with the other females, particularly with Musammat Amin Kunwar. But this feminine incompatibility is very common in most village households, especially where the proportion of female members is high and one of them rather fancies herself. Some months before, there had been a dispute between the two brothers over the inheritance of ancestral property. Their father had recently died and the elder brother was accused of having possessed himself of more than his share, particularly of some ornaments which had been worn by his mother, which belonged to the family jointly.

Bimal Prasad probably regarded his younger brother as little more than an infant. Most elder brothers in cases where the other one is too young, undertake a friendly division and distribution, sometimes even carried into formal proceedings, fraudulently conducted in the revenue courts. It was not a great matter, but the parents of Moti's wife had taken umbrage and had encouraged their daughter to demand some of these ornaments for her own use.

The dignity and patriarchal authority of Bimal Prasad had been much disturbed by this presumptuous conduct of a younger brother's wife, who occupied, at the best, a very subordinate position and who had only quite recently joined the family circle. Strained relations ensued and ultimately, at the insistence of her parents, Moti's wife had left for her parental home. But, strangely enough, it was clearly established that the feud had not affected the relations of the two brothers, who appeared to continue to be on the best of terms.

•

For some days before the tragedy, Moti had been far from well, and it was on this account that Bimal was sleeping in the same room with him. In the morning, Bimal failed to appear at his usual hour for feeding the bullocks, and no sound was heard proceeding from the room where the two men slept. Musammat Baguli seemed to be anxious as to whether anything had happened and after consulting with the other women, she pushed the door open . A ghastly spectacle met her gaze. Her son-in-law was lying dead on his charpoy in a pool of blood, his skull smashed and the head and features mercilessly lacerated. It was at once apparent that the murderer had some grudge against the deceased which he had worked off upon the body of his victim while he had him at his mercy.

Bimal Prasad had no enemy who was likely to feel like this towards him, unless it could be his brother Moti, if he had been secretly nursing a grievance over the family inheritance. A heavy chopper stained with blood lay on the blood-stained floor between the two beds. The younger brother lay on his back on the charpoy, quite motionless and apparently unconscious. On examining him closely, Musammat Baguli found that he was alive and calling the other women into the room, asked Moti what had happened. The invalid jabbered something unintelligible in reply. She shook him and asked who had killed Bimal Prasad. Moti replied that he did not know.

The women made no further search and broke out into the loud lamentations and ear-piercing cries and groans which are customary on such occasions. The sound of their dismal chorus soon brought some of the neighbours to the spot, but none of them found anything which threw further light upon the commission of the crime. No one at that time accused Moti, but it would have been strange if they had not already concluded in their own minds that he must be the culprit.

•

The village chaukidar arrived in due course, and he was shortly afterwards despatched to the nearest thana to make his report. Soon after his departure the mukhia (head man of the village) arrived and made some inquiries of his own. He is always entitled, if not expected, to assist the authorities by making inquiries into anything reflecting upon the good name of the village. He remained on guard during the interval before the arrival of the police, and eventually induced Moti to bestir himself. An ugly fact was then discovered. He had risen from his bed and sat down by the door of his room. They examined his body and under the light covering which he wore they found patches, rather than spots, of blood upon his chest and arms.

According to the mukhia and the women, he more than once, confessed to the crime, assenting to their inquiries rather than making any definite statement, except that on one occasion he added that he had killed his brother because he had deprived him of some of the property. Musammat Baguli then, informed the mukhia that she had seen Moti wandering about in the courtyard during the night. She had been asleep and had awoke on hearing his voice.

She had coughed and he had asked 'Who's that?' She had then looked up from under her quilt and had asked him what he was doing. He had answered that he had come out to answer nature's call and had lost his way back to his room. She had told him which way to go and had seen him disappear in that direction.

Musammat Pyari then, stated that the chopper belonged to her, and that she had hidden it for safety, before going to bed the night before, in the stack of chaff. The object of the midnight journey across the courtyard must have been to fetch the chopper. The Sub-Inspector thus found on his arrival an almost complete chain of circumstantial evidence already established, with a motive which, if not very strong, was quite adequate for a murder by a villager.

•

The dead body was despatched to the civil surgeon for examination. Meanwhile, Salman and the Sub-Inspector engaged Moti in conversation. This contributed nothing to the general stock of information. But so far as a formal confession was concerned, Salman did not trouble himself, as from the statements of the women, the admissions of Moti were sufficient. What troubled him more was the parlous condition of health and mind in which Moti appeared to be. He mumbled and returned incoherent answers to all questions put to him.

Salman at first thought that this was a put on, and was inclined to try and bring him to reason by a little slapping. But, he eventually became convinced that Moti was in a state of high fever, bordering on delirium. This was attributed to the strain upon his physical and mental capacity resulting from the terrible deed he had committed, and the Sub-Inspector decided that the only thing to be done was to send him straight off in custody to the hospital.

There, Moti remained for some weeks with a very serious illness, which nearly had a fatal termination. But he got over it and was committed to trial at sessions, where he was convicted of the murder of his brother and sentenced to death.

•

His family was not well enough to provide him with legal assistance, and were probably not sufficiently concerned to save him from the gallows. Under such circumstances, the local government of the province followed the humane and sometimes valuable practice of allowing the judge to provide the accused with counsel, the cost of which was to be charged to the public exchequer. Such chosen counsel were not always experienced. They were necessarily handicapped by knowing nothing of the case except what they could glean in court from the record of the proceedings before the magistrate and from the oral evidence given at the hearing at sessions.

In this particular case, everyone concerned in the trial overlooked the importance of a report which had been made by the hospital doctor to the magistrate when the accused was released from hospital. It showed that when Moti had been admitted, he was in a condition of extreme physical weakness. He had been taking little or no food for some days and his body was emaciated. The doctor had ascertained, from one of the women, that he had taken next to nothing except great quantities of water to assuage his feverish thirst. The probable reason of the failure to notice the importance of these facts was that the report was made officially to the magistrate by way of explanation of the delay in sending the accused to court for the preliminary inquiry. After perusing the document, the magistrate had ordered it to be filed. It had never been read in open court and having served its purpose, had been forgotten.

But, when the case came before the High Court for confirmation of the death sentence, attention was drawn to this report and a comparison was instituted between the violence of the blows which, as shown by the post-mortem, must have been delivered upon the body of the deceased and the feeble condition of the accused, as disclosed by the hospital report. The only thing to be done was to summon the hospital doctor and the female witnesses, and to take additional evidence.

It often happened in those days that the doctor who conducted the post-mortem examination was not examined as a witness at the trial. The supply of official doctors was limited. He could be stationed away from the court and his time was fully occupied every day, all day. If he were to attend sessions trials regularly, especially where such attendance involved two or three days' absence, the whole of his official work would be disorganised, with serious injury to the community. He is, therefore, summoned only by the judge in those cases where his presence would be urgently required. This practice was occasionally a source of embarrassment to the court of criminal appeal, particularly when some point arose which had been overlooked or inadequately dealt with in the trial court.

On this occasion, the civil surgeon could only say what appeared to be obvious on the face of it, but what had not been emphasised till now – that the victim had been killed by a number of heavy blows, delivered with great force. It looked like the work of a madman, or a man who acted in frenzy, who must have possessed a pair of strong arms. The first blow must have been delivered stealthily, and with such force and direction as to beat down any possible resistance by the deceased. This evidence given in the presence of the hospital doctor enabled the latter to express his opinion with greater confidence.

•

The surgeon elaborated in more detail the report which he had sent to the magistrate on Moti's condition when he had been brought to the hospital. He also presented the history of his fever, weakness and need of nourishment from which he was suffering at that time. He was quite positive now that Moti did not possess the requisite strength to perform the act of which he was accused of. It was not a mere question of difficulty, nor of degree, nor of a superhuman effort made in delirium. It was a physical impossibility for anyone in his condition to have made such a prolonged and resolute effort.

This, of course, was the end of the case. No court could convict of a capital charge in the face of expert medical testimony that the act of which the prisoner was accused was to him a physical impossibility. But further probing of the evidence of the women strongly supported the hospital doctor's view.

Moti had not been taking anything but water, and had been so weak that he was unable to raise himself from his charpoy without the help of a stick. He could only walk with assistance and that too with difficulty. It was quite clear that the conviction was a miscarriage of justice. It is interesting turn to some of the questions which certainly should have occurred to any investigation officer of experience when he first arrived on the scene.

How did Moti know, if he had been lying all day ill on his cot, where to find the chopper in the dark?

It had admittedly been hidden by one of the women, out of his hearing, and out of sight of his room.

Why was it hidden at all that night, close to the entrance? How had Moti got there without assistance? How was it that Musammat Baguli had not seen the chopper in his hand when she woke up? How was it that none of the women had heard a sound while the murder was being committed within a few feet at least of Musammat Amin Kunwar and her mother?

At the trial, the Sub-Inspector had said that he heard a rumour in the village, connecting the mukhia with Musammat Amin Kunwar. That was all! The mukhia had not been called as a witness, presumably because it was thought that any confession made to him by Moti would be ruled out, and the topic was not pursued.

This fact introduces a feature in village life which, though it may be rare, was not unheard of. The mukhia wielded no inconsiderable influence and authority in village life. Moreover, this particular mukhia had a reputation of his own. A few years ago, a shooting party of Englishmen were camping near the village, and they found themselves unable to procure from the village any milk or eggs or any other local produce. Their servant, after making discreet inquiries, discovered that the mukhia had given orders that none should be supplied. He was offended about something. He may have heard that the sahibs had shot a peacock or unconsciously committed some other unpardonable offence against the village sentiment. The party of Englishmen took a bold course. They came to the village and sought an interview with the mukhia, but the worthy old gentleman, who had an air of regal majesty, was adamant.

One of the English sahibs seized hold of a bucket of water which his servant had drawn from the village well, and threw it over the mukhia. It was a rather risky game to play, but it had the desired effect. The mukhia saw that the sahibs meant business. They had guns with them, and there was no saying what they might try next. He did not want to expose himself to further insult and loss of dignity in the presence of his satellites, and with heroic self-control he assured the visitors that there had been a mistake, and that the contents of the village were at their disposal. The villagers followed suit, and were only too pleased at the turn of events which enabled them to dispose of some of their saleable goods at a more than reasonable figure. Thus, the incident closed, and everyone was satisfied.

•

But, ironically, the villagers later hailed mukhia as someone who had humbled the English sahibs. The mukhia's word, up to a point, was law in the village. It was also said that if he wanted a young and attractive woman brought to his residence at night, she was brought. That could only happen when the husband was compliant. When he was not, other means were adopted. The supposition that the mukhia or someone acting on his behalf was responsible for the murder of Bimal Prasad was the only explanation which fitted the case. As it was a physical impossibility for Moti to have done it, it was superfluous to discuss the motive which might otherwise have operated upon his mind.

Leaving the outer door on the chain only may have been the regular practice, but the placing of the chopper in the stack near the entrance was significant. It seemed curious that the door of the room in which the two men were sleeping could be so easily opened in the morning. The blood patches found on Moti, though consistent with his guilt, were not inconsistent with his innocence. One would have expected to find a number of spots of varying size caused by the spurting of the blood from the body of his victim. But the patches which were found under his clothing might have been deliberately smeared. It was sure to have been done by someone who had his wits even in the moments of committing murder.

•

But perhaps the most significant incident of all was the assiduous attention of the mukhia to the scene of the crime and his taking charge in the absence of the chaukidar at the thana. There would be nothing remarkable in his visit to collect information, though it would be unusual. And if he went, he would be quite likely to try and get a statement from the inmates of the house, especially if anyone was disposed to confess his guilt. But, he would probably not go alone in the ordinary course.

If these inferences are correct, then it was certain that Musammat Baguli and her daughter and probably also the two other women, were acting in collusion with the mukhia, and could not be expected to possess the moral courage to interfere or to expose the plot. It is difficult to resist the conclusion that the sub-inspector, even if he was not behind the scenes from the first, lent himself to the plot and allowed dust to be thrown in his eyes for the usual consideration.

11

The Murder of a Mahant

A Hindu temple is an institution as well as a structure. Big or small, there is a physical building that houses the gods and goddesses where the pilgrims and the faithful come to offer prayers. Besides, there is an institution for management of affairs of the temple, comprising the *mahants* (priests), the brahmins and the others associated with the affairs of the temple. Many of the temples possess considerable wealth in the shape of landed property, jewellery, elephants, banners and other trappings embroidered.

This wealth is both inherited and steadily increased and accumulated from the daily offerings of worshippers and pilgrims, as well as from occasional legacies and endowments. The temple building is intended for the accommodation of the idol, and for the officiating mahants or managers and priests. The great majority of the temples in villages and small towns are quite small and unimposing, leaving out the exceptions. Some of the most famous temples present an appearance of great splendour.

The exterior of the temple is generally white. These small white buildings are familiar sights as one passes through villages and the open countryside where they are often quite isolated. On the other hand, many of them stand inconspicuously in the row of houses and shops in the village street and in the congested bazaars, looking almost crowded out by the buildings on either side of them. One can often catch a glimpse of a temple down a narrow side lane or *gali*, as they are called. In many of them, their small size is compensated by the wealth of decoration which has been lavished upon them. They are open to the street on all sides and seem to have no special entrance or exit.

Although the mahants and managers who live there generally have plenty of ready money and much valuable jewellery, there are few outward signs of luxury and comfort about their quarters, generally in close proximity of the main temple. Ancient books of value are preserved, wrapped in cloths or packed in boxes and no attempt is made to display anything like an imposing show of library shelves. Many of the costly and treasured ornaments are removed altogether for safe custody until they are wanted, generally on festive occasions for decoration of idols.

These temples, some of which make frequent appearances both in the civil and criminal courts, have certain peculiar characteristics. There are black sheep as well as white among the mahants and holy men. Some of them become indolent and self-indulgent. Falling into temptation, they lead somewhat dissolute lives. They are given to litigating, both in competition with other institutions and over disputes relating to the regulation of their internal and domestic affairs. Most mahants are learned and devout ascetics, with a few exceptions. These black sheep seem to devote little of their time to the moral advancement either of their fellow-men or of themselves except during great festivals.

•

Cases come to court in which breaches of a public trust are alleged against a manager of a temple, or its trust, and it is sought to remove him from office. Or when on the death of a mahant or a guru, a struggle ensues between two or more contending candidates as to which shall succeed to the office. In such cases, very serious charges of maladministration, personal indulgence, and general misconduct are freely made. There is hardly any court case in which anyone on the other side in a dispute about the affairs of a temple had a good word to say for the manager, even if he was not accused of conduct which would be outrageous to anyone.

It has always been the policy of the civil as well as police administration not to interfere with the institutions of the Hindus, Muslims, or any other religion. A case under the section relating to a public religious trust cannot be brought into court without the sanction in writing of the higher authority in government. Moreover, conduct which would usually be regarded as a breach of trust, turns out to be false. For example, in case of an endowment in which the property is left for the use of a particular priest or individual selected for the management of the temple, to be spent upon the purposes of the temple and its worship in his absolute discretion. In such cases, he is free to disburse the money almost in any way he sees fit, such as processions, celebrations, or even banquets, directly or indirectly connected with the business of the temple.

•

These priests and mahants do not marry, but they feel the need of a woman's assistance for the various purposes of domestic life, and many of them are not averse to having mistresses, who, as we shall see in the case of Bhagwan Das, are euphemistically and by courtesy, described as members of a branch of the mahant's family.

Moreover, in a place where pilgrims resort in large numbers, the conduct of a religious institution may involve the employment of a large number of touts, who are paid by a commission from the proceeds of their labours. Many families have their hereditary priests, and stick to them. But many, who go on pilgrimage for the first time, arrive at the railway station or in the town, without the least idea where to go next or what to do. The touts are eager to present their services to such pilgrims.

•

It was year 1907. In a small town of Basantpur, one morning, mahant Bhagwan Das was found murdered. The temple where the tragedy occurred was down a gali. It was one of the several temples in the same neighbourhood. There were houses and shops nearby, for the gali opened out into a substantial thoroughfare. It may not be called a road and became muddy during the rainy season. A couple of hundred metres down the gali was the police station. Plus, the area was fairly populated.

When his murder was reported, Salman took the lead on this case. During his investigation, he found out that the temple where Bhagwan Das was murdered was easily accessible from the street. The temple had a flowing income, and so did the mahant. He had a taste for the good things of life. He was unmarried, but far from being alone. In his later years, he had developed a distinct taste for 'nieces'. The gross receipts at the temple at the time of his murder were alleged to be two rupees per day. This income was largely due to the work of Bhagwan Das's touts. The receipts must have been considerably more during the festival seasons.

The 'niece', Gayatri Devi, who gave evidence at the trial, stated that the deceased mahant might have had seven thousand rupees locked in his safe. Everyone who has heard witnesses give evidence knows what *might* probably meant in such circumstances. The statement was certainly an understatement. The deceased also possessed some three thousand rupees' worth of ornaments, and guarded in the safe another collection estimated to be worth about two thousand rupees, with which he decorated the idol on auspicious occasions and which he locked up at night. He was never known to be without money or female company, which ought to have been good enough for any man, however holy. He had a content, easy and indolent existence without any fears, but he was getting infirm.

His sole anxiety was the insistence of his touts, who were accused of having murdered him. But, it was certain that their importunity for better commission did not greatly trouble him, and his conduct betrayed no sign of one who went in fear of his life. The murdered mahant Bhagwan Das, who had many rival institutions in his vicinity, had employed a large number of touts. This is an important fact to understand who had murdered him. If his touts did so, they were killing the goose which laid the golden egg. In as much as the motive of the murder was said to be loot and not a pice was stolen, the easy-going sense of security in which he lived, was a fact to be borne in mind.

His establishment consisted of the 'niece' Gayatri Devi, who was about thirty, her daughter Jaya, aged about eight, and a man-servant named Dukhhan. Formerly, there had been another 'niece', Gulabo by name, who had been succeeded by Gayatri. Dukhhan stated at the trial that Bhagwan Das had left a will by which Gulabo inherited all his possessions. This will be never forthcoming as Gayatri took possession of everything after the old man's death, including the receipts at the temple. The disposition of his property away from her negated the possibility of any motive on Gayatri's part for encompassing the old man's death; the existence of the will must have been regarded with suspicion. It was probably the suggestion of the fertile brain of Dukhhan.

The antecedents of Gayatri Devi made her presence in the temple rather interesting. She had a husband, but apparently, she had ceased to take any interest in him for some years. She had 'kept house' for more than one other man before she had been brought to the mahant. This had occurred quite recently when Gulabo had taken her departure. Gayatri Devi's own version of her presence at temple with the deceased mahant Bhagwan Das, was naive. She claimed that her husband was mad. Of course, no one could prove he wasn't, for no one had seen him. But, on account of this madness, she said that her father, who was mahant's friend had brought her to the temple so that the mahant could look after her as a daughter. She called the deceased *chacha* or uncle. This was correct, but inaccurate. Gayatri said that she did all the work of the temple, except the puja.

•

The absence of an absconding accused during the trial of a case especially criminal ones, does sometimes operate unfavourably against those who are put on their trial. Absconding is certainly not a conclusive indication of a guilty conscience. Nothing is better recognised than the natural timidity of the accused of a criminal charge, his dread as an accused person, and his foolish belief in an escape as the most efficacious method of avoiding trouble, even when he is innocent. It is his first inspiration. He soon sees a reason to regret the step. He is never happy away from his village, especially if it happens to be his ancestral home. Soon, he return, even when he is guilty, and in either case generally makes his reappearance by going straight to the magistrate's court and giving himself up.

Salman was deeply intrigued by this crime. The case against the three accused, so far as the question of motive was concerned in the murder of Bhagwan Das, was a palpably weak one. The direct evidence though superficially strong, was peculiar and suggestive, and deserved some attention in detail. It has often been pointed out that a case of circumstantial evidence is the most satisfactory of all. This is because circumstances and admitted facts speak for themselves and are unlikely to have been invented for the purpose of creating a false case. If they fit into the framework of the story, they create a chain of testimonies which holds everything together.

But, the value of a case of circumstantial evidence is not always understood by the police or appreciated by those who are concerned in fixing a crime on the right person. The consequence is that a fairly strong case of circumstantial evidence is ruined by the introduction of direct testimony which is palpably false. Also, it is characteristic of several trails. This is called 'police padding'.

Many witnesses suffer from enthusiasm. This seems to increase their mendacity. They do not like facts to speak for themselves. Rather, they like to do the talking, and often seem to be convinced that they can produce the desired result. It is rare for a sessions judge to criticise witnesses or comment upon their evidences. The judge is generally occupied in typing or writing the evidences, and he is not unlikely to be told by the defence counsel, that he is interfering with the course of justice. A proof is hardly ever taken of their evidences before they give it. The standpoint of the police is somewhat different, though they are often confirmed optimists. But, they have behind them training and experience and the recollection of past failures.

They have seen generations of lawyers on the bench in the court of appeal, weighing the details of the evidence like a goldsmith with the grains of gold in his delicate scales, and ultimately spoiling the case by finding some so-called 'weak link' in the beautiful chain which spread itself before the eyes of the keen inspector.

A confession is the best of all! With some such idea as this, an eyewitness is often dragged in to supplement and sometimes to destroy a well-balanced case of circumstantial evidence.

•

The main story in the temple murder case was related by Dukhhan and confirmed by Gayatri, and in some small degree by the youthful Jaya. There were discrepancies in details that delighted the cross-examiner, that is the defence counsel, and attracted the attention of the court. But it was not a case in which discrepancies in details were of much consequence. If the story was true, it all happened so quickly and in such a confined space that accurate observations were hardly possible. The real question was whether there could possibly be any truth in it at all.

Dukhhan said that one evening, early in the month of September at about 7:00 p.m., six men who worked as touts for Bhagwan Das and whom he had named in the FIR, including the three who were on their trial, came to the temple to have a talk with Bhagwan Das. They all sat down together with the four inmates of the temple. The *chilam* (pipe) was produced, and smoking was indulged in. Conversations, as usual, turned upon the money which was coming in, and about the share of the touts, but there was no quarrel or dispute, until the men leapt to their feet and went for the throat of Bhagwan Das in a fit of rage.

Four of them, including Mahadeo and Ram Charan, attacked his arms and held them firmly, while Sital Prasad, in whose hands Dukhhan said he saw a knife, attacked the mahant. The sixth went to the doorway and barred the exit from the inner room in which they were. Dukhhan grappled with the man nearest to him and felt a sudden stab in his stomach from a small dagger. Although surrounded, he was able to see Sital Prasad attacking the mahant with the knife which he held in his hand. But either the attack upon himself was the feeblest ever delivered by four men upon an undefended one, or he was able to perform a feat of incredible pluck and agility. He 'removed' the knife from his stomach and the hand that held it, and made for the door. Dashing past the man who stood there and who caught hold of his leg, he got out through the temple onto the road. Here, he found four men, who were also touts, waiting for him. He managed to dodge past them, and raced at full speed up the gali onto the main thoroughfare. Now, it was necessary to have some men there, waiting for him. The gang's plan of campaign, as outlined in his graphic account, was to overpower Dukhhan and put him out of action either for resistance or alarm. The other three inmates were, at best, a weak body and could be dealt with at leisure. But, it was essential that there should be no escape and no opportunity for anyone to give an alarm.

•

Dukhhan's description of his marvellous escape read like the account of a famous run by a star Rugby football three-quarter who manages suddenly to get away with the ball, and either throws off or outpaces all who try to collar him. The main difference is that in Dukhhan's case, he had to run straight down a very narrow lane, through four men who were drawn up in waiting for him. He could neither side step nor trick them, and he had a hole in his stomach which must have been bleeding profusely and causing him pain. He declared that he lost much blood but nothing stopped his heroics as bleeding and shouting 'Murder!' and 'Loot!' He ran the distance of nearly half a mile, through the gali, on to the main thoroughfare, and reached the police station without having been seen or heard by a single soul. If this performance was to be accepted in the trial court, one can only say that truth is indeed stranger than fiction.

On his arrival at the police station, he was very exhausted and fell unconscious for some time. It was after almost an hour that he got life back in him and he could make his report. When he said that he was sufficiently recovered, he made his report which was a curious one. He mentioned vaguely about the existence of an ill-feeling between the mahant and the touts, whose names and family details he gave to the police. But, he made no mention of any attempt at looting. The main charge which he made and which was entertained by the police was one of an attempt to murder him, which had only been prevented by his flight. He added that the mahant and Gayatri had been beaten.

•

In view of what he asked the court subsequently to believe, this report was a condensed one and contained many omissions. In the first place, it did not say that he had seen one of the persons named using a knife upon the mahant. This was a curious omission. If his story was true, it can only be explained by his ignorance of what had actually happened to Bhagwan Das. He himself explained his silence by saying that he was suffering too severely from his wound to be able to give vivid details when at the police station.

This was followed by another strange feature in the report, and to the equally strange conduct of the Sub-Inspector who took charge of the case. In the report, there was no specific reference to his own wound. If it was only a slight one and self-inflicted, this was perfectly natural. He left it quite vague so that it would be open to anyone afterwards to say that, so far as the report was concerned, it was quite conceivable that not only the attempt to kill him, but even the attempt to stab him had failed. He had not pinned himself to the existence of a serious wound. But, he made it quite clear to the Sub-Inspector that he was much shaken and ill and also in pain. The Sub-Inspector asked him if he wished to go to hospital and he declined. This is not something unusual. Most victims almost always decline at first, even if they afterwards consent, unless they realise that their condition is critical. But, as he was reporting a case of an attempt to murder himself and had certainly made statements which suggested that he had been stabbed while he had arrived not merely out of breath but in such a condition that he could not make a report at all for nearly an hour, the Sub-Inspector's failure to ask whether he had received any wound and what its nature was, or to ask to be allowed to see the condition of the man's body at the place where an attempt had been made to stab him, is quite unintelligible. No one ever saw the hole in Dukhhan's stomach, or the injuries which he said he received, when they were fresh.

After Dukhhan had made his report, he went back to the temple with the Sub-Inspector. The discoveries made on their arrival demanded close attention. The mahant was lying dead. He had been stabbed in twelve places. Afterwards, it appeared that two blows had penetrated the heart and two to the right lung. There were no signs upon his body of his having struggled with his assailant. He had been despatched deliberately, and probably treacherously, in cold blood. Gayatri Devi had some slight superficial wounds, or rather cuts, upon the stomach. Dukhhan declared at the trial that he saw her stabbed in the stomach. This was a serious addition to his first story. It was quite inconsistent with the report of 'beating', an expression which had also been used in the report made at the police station. Its omission from the report, if it was true, seems to be unintelligible.

•

Neither Dukhhan nor Gayatri Devi was medically examined until the next day, when the magistrate began to entertain doubts about parts of the story. But, the opinion of the doctor was that neither of them had been stabbed, and the alleged attempt to kill either of them was illusory. This was another point which deserved consideration. No one with, much experience of crime, would doubt that in the majority of cases, if ten men had decided to kill the mahant in the temple, they would not think of adding the murder of Dukhhan, Gayatri Devi and the child Jaya to their other crime, if only for the purpose of destroying all possibility of their being identified by an eyewitness. The more one considered it, the more incredible it seems that Dukhhan should not have been murdered at once before anything else was attempted.

A bloodstained knife was found in the temple that evening. Its ownership was never established. The medical expert said that it might have been responsible for all the wounds on the corpse as well as for those on the survivors. At the trial, the prosecution rather committed itself to this theory. This was a palpable fallacy, which Dukhhan himself rejected, because he finally declared that he saw both the deceased and the woman stabbed during the attack upon himself. It would therefore follow that there must have been more than one knife. But, unless it was a knife which belonged to the temple and could be identified, why should ten assailants want to leave one of the knives behind?

Still more remarkable were the discoveries made the next morning by Gayatri Devi. When she was cleaning, she found an umbrella under the *takht* (wooden platform of the temple). Inside the umbrella was the sheath of a dagger, which accounted for a second weapon, and which corresponded to that which Dukhhan said had been used upon him. Even the Sub-Inspector was sceptical about this discovery. He declared that, in accordance with his duty, he had made a thorough search the night before, and had seen nothing of the kind. But, if he had searched, it would have been almost impossible to have overlooked such an object as an umbrella. He would not say that he himself had searched beneath the takht, though he certainly ought to have done so. It is true that it was the rainy season and that any visitor to the temple might have been carrying an umbrella.

But why should one of the alleged murderers want to hide it at all? And further, why should he put a dagger sheath inside it? Neither the umbrella nor the sheath was ever identified as the property of any known person and the prosecution contented itself with making the point that if two knives had been used, they must have been brought into the building, as they did not belong there.

Gayatri Devi said at the trial that she saw the umbrella in the hand of one of the accused who was missing. There was no trace of any attempt to break open any of the temple boxes, and nothing had been stolen. This made the case against the touts more mysterious than ever. They knew that there was a good deal of valuable stuff inside the premises, and they had at least an hour to ransack the place. According to Gayatri Devi, the assailants had left her for dead. She had thought that her last hour had come, and had become unconscious. This could not possibly have been caused by any of the injuries she had received, though in the case of a less hardened woman of the world, it might have occurred from fright and shock. She had cried out for help before fainting, but no one was forthcoming who had heard any cry at this stage.

The little girl Jaya corroborated the story told by her mother and Dukhhan but although she knew the men by sight, they left her alone, and she said that she escaped to another inner room and hid herself.

•

When Gayatri Devi recovered and found herself still alive, she ran out on to the roof and gave an alarm, calling out, "They have killed!" This brought to the scene two witnesses who gave curious evidence. Their two stories corresponded very closely, although they did not happen to see one another. Both of them complained that they could not see well at night.

One of them had happened to pass the temple a little while before he heard the cries of Gayatri Devi on the roof, and had seen four men standing in the gate, but he was not prepared to say that he recognised them. Both of these witnesses went out upon hearing Gayatri's cries, but they were discouraged from going to the temple to see what was the matter, because as soon as they got outside their houses, they were greeted with showers of stones and brickbats. They could not say who threw them, but they were both certain that there were ten men in all, and that they also looked like the touts who frequently visited the temple when the mahant was alive.

•

This evidence was open to several comments. It was a singular coincidence that both men should have behaved in precisely the same way. They came from slightly different directions, although at much about the same time and yet, both were assailed by all ten throwing missiles. Neither of them was prepared to identify anyone, but each gave the same description. Neither had the courage to brave the storm and go to the woman's assistance. Both concluded that it was none of their business. But both stories seem incredible, on the face of it.

Why should men who had already committed a murder wait upon the spot while the woman gave an alarm in order to stone everyone who came at her cries? The probability was that these two witnesses were what is known as 'mere police padding'.

The three men – Mahadeo, Ram Charan and Sital Prasad – were convicted. They appealed in the High Court, and it was held that there were so many points about the evidence which required further elucidation that the conviction must be set aside, and a new trial was ordered. At the second trial, which took place before an experienced English Sessions judge, they were acquitted. One of the assessors at the first trial volunteered the opinion that Dukhhan and Gayatri Devi were accomplices, though the point had not been suggested. He may have thought that they were the principals and got some bazaar ruffians to come in and carry out the murder for them. Or he may have thought that it had all been arranged by the other 'niece' Gulabo, with their connivance.

It is a nice question whether upon their own statements and the circumstantial evidence available, a sufficient case to hold together in a court of law could have been constructed against them. But they were never put upon their trial, and the murderers of mahant Bhagwan Das went unpunished.

12

Running Amuck

Running amuck is a more or less dangerous frenzy, induced by a vitiated, supersensitive state of the mind. It is peculiar among such emotional people as those of the Malay Archipelago.

The word 'amuck' itself is derived from the Malaysian 'amok', which means to kill. The principal causes for this calamitous distemper may be attributed to religious hallucination, jealousy, a yearning for revenge and temporary insanity brought on by overindulgence in intoxicants, opium, or other drugs of an inflammatory nature. During ordinary times, when an amuck-runner comes out on the war-path, he is generally under the influence of religious beliefs or feeling of extreme personal vengeance.

At many places in India, a milder version of running amuck is to be found in several places. But the most important feature of this is its being prolonged, sometimes for generations, and often being calculated. Factional fights have always been a common feature in Indian villages. Local feuds, which are certain to break out into violence and bloodshed, differ fundamentally from the sudden and temporary quarrels which arise out of cattle-trespass, irrigation, jealousy and connubial infidelity. They go deeper, are more calculated and last longer. They are often handed on from one generation to another. They are not necessarily communal, though they are not always free from communal animus. They belong to a class of party warfare in the social life of the community which is probably inherent in the habits and customs of the people. They may be due to the hostility, original or inherited, of two rival local zamindars, each struggling to assert his superiority over the other.

•

In one of the conversations which Salman had with one of the native members of the village, he got to know that every Indian, from the highest to the lowest, has his *izzat* or name, to keep up. After his son, it is his most cherished possession, and if it is injured, he is an unhappy man. And in such a sensitive race, there is nothing easier to injure than the izzat. The injury may be purely imaginary, but it is keenly felt.

A zamindar whose izzat has been hurt thinks that he has lost ground with the highest authorities in his district. And if he really has, woe betide him! Moreover, he will neither forget it nor forgive the man who did it.

A big zamindar was once asked why he was content with such a small return from his wealth, which was all land, and which involved constant troubles and anxieties with his tenants as well as with his agent or *karinda*, when he could get a much bigger income by investing in some of the many successful industries. His reply was immediate and instructive. Paraphrased into English, his reply was:

> "Income is not everything. I would have to give up much of my land. My neighbour would certainly buy it to his own advantage. I would lose many tenancies and tenants. My men and followers would decrease in number and my local position would suffer. Where would my party be?"

In a word, his izzat would be injuriously affected.

And amidst his tenantry and circle of villages, there is one village which to him is above and beyond all, both in importance and in sentiment – the ancestral village. Therefore, when his rival zamindar begins to assert himself, to gain in izzat, he is deeply offended. It is a grievance to be nursed and he is ready to fight for his rights and to resist the least attack, however small and indirect, upon his possessions and authority. Thus, it often happens that between two neighbouring landowners there exists the deadliest rivalry and hatred. When two ancestral homes clash, there is bound to be trouble. The district magistrate awaits the outbreak with amused curiosity and anxiety because it will probably appear where and when it is least expected.

This hostility, which may have begun with their ancestors, invariably permeates the tenantry and the servants, all of whom form a party around their zamindari and manifest their feelings towards the members of the other party in numerous ways in their daily life. Some dispute or argument may occur over a field or some matter of cultivation, or even over a purchase which each of the two zamindars is anxious to secure for himself. A word of abuse or assault upon some quite insignificant servant will follow. No member of a party is insignificant for the purpose of giving or receiving offence. At once the case is taken into a criminal court and fought with deadly determination and often with much expenditure upon lawyers, before the magistrate. Witnesses are multiplied and once they have appeared in the array of either one side or the other, they are forever stamped with the party label. The incident will be brought up against them in cross-examination on every future occasion, however independent they may really be.

The zamindar on the losing side loses izzat, as well as a good deal of cash, and the animosity becomes more acute. "I will see you another day!" is the usual form of salutation which is generally construed as a threat to murder. It is exchanged between the karindas, who enter thoroughly in the spirit of the fight.

Contrary to the practice in ordinary theatrical performances, the principals do not usually appear. In many cases, one never sees the rival zamindars who are really responsible for the fight. They would lose izzat by appearing in court. The history of most party factions is plentifully illustrated by litigation, which is sometimes the sole occupation. It is certainly the most absorbing interest in the lives of many zamindars. The hostility may be of modern growth.

As every reader knows, many villages are split up into shares, which are held by various shareholders. One may have fallen on evil days, and mortgaged his share to a moneylender, or to a successful commercial man possessed of cash and desirous of acquiring land and local influence. A mortgage suit is brought, a decree is obtained, and the share passes into the hands of the new man. Shareholders of villages do not welcome strangers in their circle. Out of this small beginning, a long future of bitter feud may be confidently predicted. Or it may happen that two otherwise friendly and aristocratic zamindars of high caste and ancient lineage will fall out over a woman.

One might multiply the causes and variations of mental temperature by copious illustrations. But the result is generally the same – a crime of violence, sooner or later.

On a crime being committed, an experienced police officer will never fail to inquire what factions, or parties exist in the village. These village factions are the most prolific of all the causes which give birth to false reports and accusations so constantly made, to which many devote themselves with the skill and enthusiasm which others will bestow upon a favourite game.

When a village feud of this kind exists, the task of an officer investigating a village crime is anything but an enviable one, except when a death has occurred. Even then, there are sometimes insuperable difficulties.

Whatever divisions exist among the villagers, if someone is murdered in a fight, everyone agreed that one death amongst the community is enough, and that another at the hands of the hangman is to be avoided at all costs.

•

Early one morning, at around 2 a.m., one Chaman, a cultivator of the *faquir* caste, arrived at the thana with his companions. He had come from Anrakas village which was some ten miles away from the thana. He had a sad tale to narrate. He said that there had existed in the village, for some considerable time, great enmity between his zamindar Jaswant Singh and another zamindar. He and his friends had been persecuted and threatened by the rival faction of Jaswant Singh, including six of his *lathials* (stick wielders) whom he also named. He mentioned that they had been joined by others in the village whom they had persuaded to side with them. He went on to state that, for the sake of troubling him, the others had recently collected and continued to store an offensive heap of manure and refuse outside his house. They had constantly been asked to stop storing the stuff there as it was of no special advantage to them. Their sole object was to annoy and insult. He, along with his brother, and others living in the adjoining houses had all protested, but without avail.

On the previous evening, Musammat Badamo, the mother of one of his neighbours, had come to throw rubbish on the heap, and had been rebuked by Nathia, Chaman's wife. According to Chaman's report, Badamo had then broken out into *gaali* or abuse. It is difficult to convey an accurate impression of what this means.

Some village women's voice suddenly becomes harsh and rasping. They begin shouting abuses at the top of their power. This immediately provokes a similar outburst from their opponent, and is followed by a rapidly rising crescendo, until it seems that one of them must break a blood vessel. Their fluency is extraordinary. They are never at a loss for words. Nothing will stop them and they seldom pause to take a breath.

A large number of sudden fights which end in murder begin with a mild outbreak of abuse of this kind over a mere trifle. Sometimes, an unfortunate husband who returns tired and hungry from a long day in the fields, looking forward to his evening meal and a quiet rest, is goaded into madness. Upon losing self-control, he resorts to violence, in turn inflicting serious injuries, and even death, upon his wife. Chaman reported that, owing to the replies made by Nathia, his wife to Badamo. Badamo's son came up and gave Nathia a full-blooded blow on her nose. Nathia immediately retired to her house, weeping. Chaman came out to the rubbish heap and rebuked the young man for his brutality. Thereupon, Badamo's son lifted his lathi and struck him a hard blow.

Then, a large number of men came up from the side of Badamo to support the assailant. Chaman named six of his male neighbours and four women, who proceeded to belabour the unfortunate Chaman and his brother Aman, who came to his assistance. Chaman said that he was attacked and knocked about as he lay on the ground in a bleeding and semi-unconscious condition. Seeing the plight in which he lay, his old mother-in-law, Musammat Kapuri flung herself upon Chaman, in the hope of saving his life. She received the remainder of the blows which were meant for Chaman and she finally succumbed to her injuries.

•

This is by no means unusual in village fights. Quite an appreciable number of women have been killed in this way. Chaman recorded the charge of the murder of his mother-in-law by the six men whom he named, along with four women at the station. About two hours after Chaman had finished his report, a number of sympathisers from the rival group arrived from the village, accompanied by the chaukidar. They made a report against Chaman and Aman, and some of their relations, for rioting and unlawful assembly, combined with personal violence and injuries inflicted upon some of them.

It is a singular feature about these occasions when, after a village quarrel, both sides appear at the police station to make a report against their respective opponents. The truth is often found to lie with the side which is late in reaching the station. This may be due to the fact that their injuries are more severe, and that it has taken them longer to get a sufficient number of people who are willing to make the journey to the nearest thana. It may be due to the fact that they delay in order to secure the attendance of the village chaukidar, or due to the fact that the party who is making a false report also make special efforts to be first in the field. On this occasion, the sub-inspector had already left for the scene of crime when the second party arrived which is why he was not aware of the second report.

On his arrival in the village, he proceeded straight to Chaman's house. It would be too much to say that an investigating officer arriving to make an inquiry in an Indian village was ever surprised at anything, but what he saw was different from what he had expected to see.

The notorious rubbish-heap stood some little distance away from the entrance to the block of dwellings where Chaman lived. He found no bloodstains there. The rapidity with which these are removed, and with which all signs of washing are dried up by the sun, constantly increases the difficulty of detective work, especially where there has been a party fight.

Members of the police force are hardly ever within reach when a crime has been committed, and much can be done before they can be fetched from the nearest thana. The villagers are generally so connected, directly or indirectly, by ties of blood, marriage, or interest with both sets of combatants that plenty can be found to confuse the traces, while none are concerned to stop this interference with the course of justice. Further, the *mukhiya* and the chaukidar are so often committed to one of the sides that their report of what they observed when they reached the spot can seldom be trusted.

•

What was more remarkable was that no signs of any recent struggle could be detected. The house occupied by Chaman was one of a little knot of buildings which might all be part of one dwelling with several doors, but which were in fact separate houses. The principal entrance to it was through an opening in a mud wall, leading into a fair-sized courtyard in which stood a neem tree. Aman, Chaman's brother, lived with his family in one of these houses, and Wazir Ali lived with his family in another. The dead body of the old woman was lying inside the courtyard, close to the neem tree. Patches of blood were found under the tree, and there was a considerable quantity of blood on the ground where the body lay.

An examination of the route from the rubbish-heap to the entrance disclosed nothing, and the soil did not look as though anything had been done to clean it. On examining the body, the Sub-Inspector found that it had been almost pulverised and bore several wounds, which must have been inflicted by a series of smashing blows. It appeared to him that these were similar to the case of a person who had been killed accidentally, unless her assailants had vindictively beaten the life out of her. Perhaps, it continued to deface and destroy the frame even after death. But, he also noticed injuries which could hardly be accounted for by blows, in particular, marks on the neck, as if something had been pressed tightly into the skin. This suggested strangling. It was clearly a perfect case for a post-mortem examination so he despatched the body in the charge of one of his constables to the civil surgeon.

Salman, along with the Sub-Inspector, took the statements of Musammat Nathia, Aman, Aman's wife, and Wazir Ali. He obtained the names of some alleged eyewitnesses but found that their stories did not come in together, although they were so vague that no alternative explanation of the crime suggested itself. Several of them agreed in stating that the old woman had not been present at any time during the fight.

Finally, someone happened to mention that she was nearly blind and needed assistance when she walked about. His growing doubts as to the truth of the story told by Chaman now strengthened into absolute scepticism. After a while, chaukidar Ram Das appeared, stating that he had just returned from the thana. He reported that they had gone there to make a report to the police of a riot and a series of injuries committed by the party to which Chaman belonged. He explained that there were two factions in the village and each was led by a rival zamindar.

Chaukidar Ram Das himself had not been in the village at the time of the fight. He had returned at about half-past nine in the evening and had heard about it. He had gone to the spot, but no traces of the recent fight could be found. He had entered Chaman's compound and there he had seen Musammat Nathia, with her now deceased mother, Musammat Kapuri, sitting under a neem tree near the house. Wazir Ali's wife was lying on the ground. Nathia had told him that the latter was unconscious, and could not speak.

Ram Das had also seen Chaman, who had a wound on his head. He added that he had afterwards seen Chaman and Wazir Ali, going in the direction of Jaswant Singh's house, the zamindar who was at the head of their faction. He had then, gone home and taken his food, which accounted for an interval of about two hours, and had left for the thana about midnight. He had not gathered sufficient information himself to make a report, but he had heard that Chaman and a few others of Jaswant Singh's followers had already gone there. Ram Das followed Chaman to the thana, and had arrived after the Sub-Inspector had left for his village. They had been told at the thana what Chaman had already reported. He had immediately left the thana again for the village.

•

Ram Das' account of what had happened in the village was hearsay, but the statement that he had himself seen Musammat Kapuri alive after the fight was over, and that Chaman and Wazir Ali appeared to have visited Jaswant Singh before going to make the first report were important developments which could hardly be inventions.

The whole story seemed straightforward enough, and it confirmed the Sub-Inspector's suspicions that he had been started upon a false scent.

It necessitated a departure upon a new line of investigation. He sent Ram Das off to find the lathials of the rival faction of zamindar Jaswant Singh on their return from the thana, and to bring them to him. When the lathials arrived, the Sub-Inspector held a sort of panchayat (village meeting) under a tree, with some of those who had taken part in the fight and other witnesses, all gathered around him. By degrees, he extracted what appeared to be the true story.

•

There had been a big row in which lathi blows had been exchanged. That was all. The parties had been separated, and no lives had been lost, nor had any serious injuries been inflicted. It had arisen out of an incident so trivial that it seemed incredible that any fight could have resulted. Some boys had been playing a game called *dudwa*. It had developed into a quarrel. A boy had slapped Sher Ali, Wazir Ali's son, who had cried and called his father. Phul Singh, a peaceable and respectable old villager had witnessed this from his house. He had come up and separated the boys. For this well-intentioned act of intervention, Phul Singh was struck on the head by Wazir Ali. Phul Singh asked him why he hit an old man, so Wazir Ali struck him again in order to enforce his argument, calling out to Chaman and Aman to come to his aid.

A verbal duel followed, and one by one, like snails after a summer shower, various members of the rival factions came out. Everyone knows what this means. The original cause of the dispute was of no consequence to any of them. They only saw a chance of supporting their friends, and of dealing a blow at their enemies.

The last to arrive knew least about it, but were the hottest in the fight. The air became thick with abuses and blood began to flow. Eventually, a separation of the combatants was affected, though with as little cause as that which had brought them together.

Both parties left the field much dissatisfied at the cessation of hostilities, and with the inconclusive nature of the finish. The only thing left to either party now, according to the ordinary rules of the game, was to get the other side implicated in a criminal case. If there is one thing in which the villager has more faith than in anything else, it is in the power of the criminal courts to do justice. The only form of justice in which he believes is the vindication of the rights of his own side. This is not necessarily a narrow view, because whatever his own side may have done is quickly forgotten. And, it is certain that the other side has been guilty of more than one act of injustice in the past which is never likely to be forgotten.

•

The rival faction of Jaswant Singh's side went off, breathing threats, and promising to launch a case of violence and robbery against the other party. The threat was absurd and was not likely to be carried out. But Chaman was not to be outdone. There had been an undoubted riot, and the infliction of serious injuries might easily be charged against himself and his friends. Rigorous imprisonment, the Indian equivalent of 'hard labour', was not an impossibility. He thought about it and decided to douse fire with fire – a criminal case to counter a possibility of criminal case against him. If the criminal law was what the rival faction wanted, they should have it. He had the usual belief in his ability to persuade the tribunal. His mother-in-law was old, feeble and blind, and a burden upon him. She might be willing to sacrifice herself in such a cause.

In this respect, he may not have exaggerated her heroism in his report, though it is improbable that he consulted her.

So Chaman, Aman, and Wazir Ali murdered the old woman in her home, in the presence of her daughter and under the sacred neem tree. They strangled her with a string; they knelt upon her breast till her poor old bones broke under the pressure; and they belaboured her head and her body with lathis. No one came forward either to try to save the wretched old victim, or to denounce the foul crime. One eye-witness professed to have seen nearly the whole thing, but it was doubtful whether he was telling the truth. The post-mortem fully established the manner of her death and there was enough circumstantial evidence to seal the fate of the three culprits, who were sentenced to death.

The strength of the case for the prosecution lay in the palpable honesty of the chaukidar and the straightforward manner in which he gave his evidence. This is a great asset because it would be clear to everyone that a case of this sort causes considerable anxiety to the trial court. There is not unlikely to be a good deal of false swearing and inconsistency of detail in the evidence.

There was nothing to show that Chaman had consulted Jaswant Singh, the zamindar, before he had murdered his mother-in-law. There would have been no time. But, it is a fair assumption that a decision had been previously come to on the point, against the contingency of a favourable occasion arising for planting a false charge of murder upon some of the opposing party. This is the only plausible explanation of the fact that Chaman went out of his way and risked the delay to pay his visit to Jaswant Singh before going to the thana to make his false report. He probably wanted to know whether he could still count upon Jaswant Singh's support, and required some assistance in framing the report which he was to make. Jaswant Singh would almost certainly suggest the addition of names of his enemies who might well have been present, even if they were not, and who might as well be hanged for other misdeeds if not for that.

A petition on behalf of the accused for pardon or commutation of the death sentence was rejected by the governor of the province. In accordance with the prescribed procedure, it was then forwarded to His Excellency, the Viceroy.

Every condemned man in British India has two independent sources to which he could appeal for the exercise of the prerogative of mercy. The Viceroy in this case commuted the death sentence of each of the three men to transportation for life. No reasons were published, nor was it required to be.

Glossary

1.	Angan	–	inner quadrangular court of the dwelling
2.	Badmash	–	bad element
3.	Baithaki	–	place in his residence where a zamindar usually sits to talk with visitors, and to transact business
4.	Bhusa	–	hay
5.	Chacha	–	uncle
6.	Charpoy	–	string cot
7.	Chaukidar	–	watchman
8.	Chilam	–	pipe
9.	Chowraha	–	crossing
10.	Dai	–	nurse
11.	Dak Gadi	–	mail carriage
12.	Daroga	–	Station House Officer
13.	Durbar	–	gatekeeper
14.	Gaali	–	abuse
15.	Gali	–	a narrow lane
16.	Huqqa	–	smoking pipe
17.	Izzat	–	name or honour
18.	Jalvahak	–	water carrier
19.	Karinda	–	agent
20.	Kotwal	–	Station House Officer (SHO)

21. Kulhari – axe
22. Lathi – a heavy, iron–bound bamboo stick
23. Lathials – stick weilders
24. Lota – water jug
25. Mahant – priest
26. Mashal – a primitive sort of torch composed of filthy rags bound around a bamboo stick
27. Mohalla – immediate neighbourhood
28. Moonshee – language instructor
29. Mufti – civil dress
30. Muharrir – police clerk/ police writer
31. Mukhiya – head man of the village
32. Nain – female member of the barber class
33. Nallah – ditch
34. Palki dak – palanquin
35. Peshbandi – the preparation of an argument in advance to meet an anticipated emergency
36. Pultoon – regiment
37. Purdah – veil
38. Sadhu – ascetic
39. Sahukar – money lender
40. Takht – the wooden platform of the temple
41. Thana – police station
42. Ticca Gadi – a four-wheeler
43. Vakil – lawyer
44. Zenana – women quarters

List of Acronyms

1.	FIR	–	First Information Report
2.	SHO	–	Station House Officer
3.	SI	–	Sub-Inspector
4.	SP	–	Superintendent of Police